Pats and Praises

143 Reproducible Patterns
to Build Self Esteem
in the Classroom

written and illustrated by Mary Strohl and Susan Schneck

SCHOLASTIC
PROFESSIONAL BOOKS

New York ■ Toronto ■ London ■ Aukland ■ Sydney

About the Authors:

When Susan Schneck and Mary Strohl met at a major children's publishing company, little did they realize they would one day own a company together. Mary, an experienced editor and former teacher trained Susan, a former teacher with an art background to work with her on her product lines. They were responsible for creating a variety of formats including dimensional paper play sets, boxed activities, learning card games, preschool activity formats, and workbooks for educational products. Ready to strike out on their own, in 1986 they became partners in their own freelance company, *Flights of Fancy*. Sharing a keen sense of design, a philosophy that learning should be fun as well as stimulating and a goal of being totally involved in the creative process of publishing, Mary and Susan have developed a fully operational studio with in-house writing, design and computer typesetting. As far as *Flights of Fancy's* future is concerned, the sky's the limit!

To Robert, whose constant support and encouragement
have kept me from crash-landing!
Susan

To Harlan, who for 20 years has helped me to "Go for it!"
Mary

ISBN: 0-590-49071-0

12 11 10 9 8 7 6 5 4 3 2 1   0 1 2 3 4 5/9

Printed in the U.S.A.

Table of Contents

Introduction

Everyone needs praise now and then, especially young students. ***Pats and Praises*** is designed to help you give praise and postive reinforcement easily without taking too much time away from your busy teaching schedule. Children flourish in a positive learning environment and they need to learn the skills to work well independently or together in groups. Strive to keep classroom spirits up and to instill enthusiasm for learning by helping children set goals and receive awards for progress toward those goals. These simple rewards will help students see their steps toward success in personal or group performance.

Chapters One through Four include a variety of reinforcement materials and displays to hold students' interest throughout the year. All the pages are reproducible with various high interest and seasonal themes that carry through each of the chapters. The index in the back of the book will help you find all the materials.

Themes Used Throughout the Book:

123	Circus Parade	Music
ABC	Cowboys/Wild West	Pelican/Seashore
Artist with Easel	Dinosaurs	Sharing Time
Astronauts/Space	Fairy Tales	Shipmates
Beehive/Flowers	Holidays	Sports
Chef/Cooking	Mountain Climbers	Whiz Kids/Feelings

Using the coordinating materials in various chapters will give your program or unit of study a uniform look that will be easily identifiable to students involved in specific projects. Use different themes for different units throughout the year or mix and match them as you like.

Some pages have color, cut and paste activities that children can complete on their own as a reward for good work or behavior. Or you may want to assemble the project yourself to give special praise to children who are making an effort to improve. Follow the assembly diagrams for each project. Children will take extra pride in showing their work when you have praised it.

The beginning of each chapter gives suggestions for using the materials provided, but we hope you'll find your own special ways of using them to enhance curriculum and classroom decor and to keep enthusiasm and spirits up throughout the school year.

Reproducing the Materials in Pats and Praises

Reproduce any of the activities for your classroom on duplicating equipment such as the thermographic copier or fluid duplicator.

If you need larger images for bulletin boards, wall charts or door displays, use an overhead or opaque projector to enlarge the art provided. Make a copy of the page to avoid show-through from the other side of the page. For best results put a black sheet of construction paper in back of the the desired page before copying. For an overhead projector make a transparency of the copy, then project it onto a large piece of paper and trace the art. The opaque projector does not require a transparency. Follow the same tracing procedure.

Chapter 1: Great Work Displays

Use the pages in this chaper as "frames" for displaying a child's work on bulletin boards or at home. All the frames can be used either horizontally or vertically, depending on the page to be framed. They are easy enough for children to color and assemble or you can make them for children as special rewards for their work. Teachers aren't the only judges of good work. Children know when they have made a special effort. Let them choose the papers that they feel should be framed for display for certain projects.

The frames can also be used on folders for work accomplished over several days or weeks. Fold a large sheet (12" x 18") of construction paper in half and glue the frame to the front and insert papers inside to send home to parents or to have available at conferences or parents night at school. The main idea is to help children take pride in a job well done and motivate them to try to do their best at all times.

123 Math

Reproduce, color, cut out and assemble as shown.

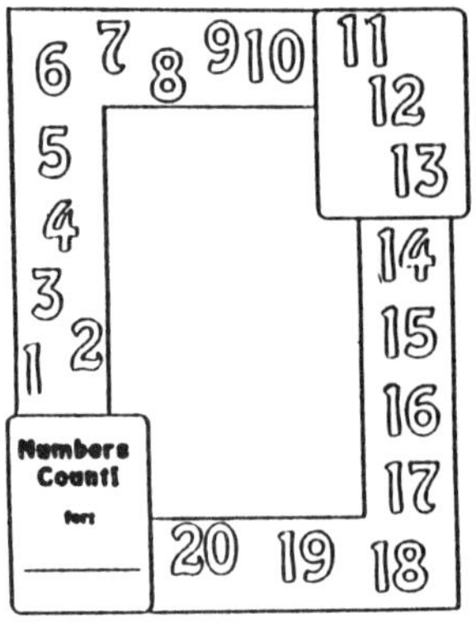

Numbers Count!
for:
_____

11 12 13

14 15 16 17 18

20 19

14 15 16 17

20 19 18

Numbers Count!

for:

_____

ABC Letter

Reproduce, color, cut out and
assemble as shown.

G H I J K L M N
F   O P
E   Q R
D   S
C   T
B   U
A   V
We
love   Z Y X W V
our
ABC'S

Q R S T U U

M N O P

Z Y X W V

We
love
our
ABC'S

name

Artist and Easel

Reproduce, color, cut out and
assemble as shown.

Brushing Up on Basics

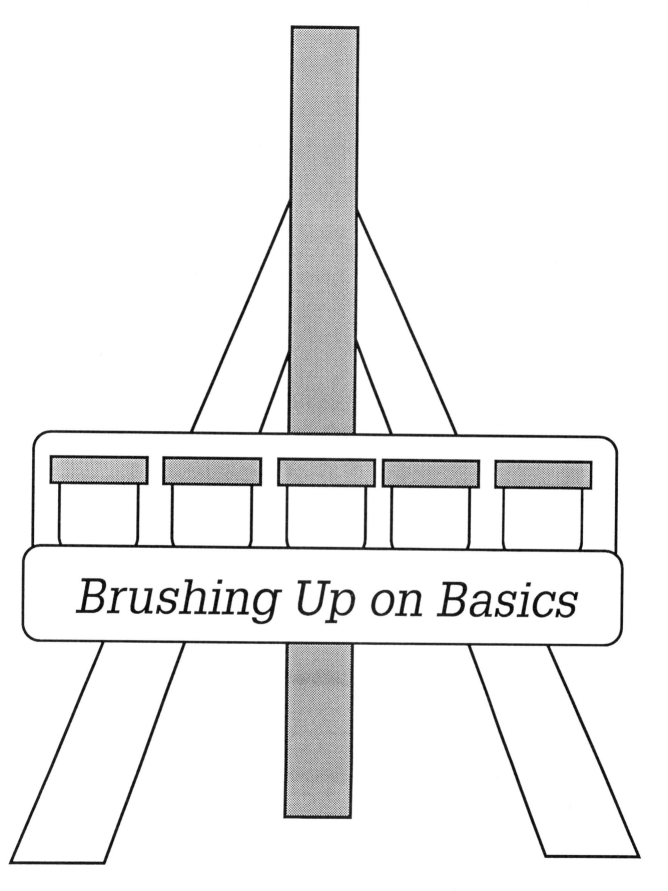

Brushing Up on Basics

Sports

Reproduce, color, cut out and
assemble as shown.

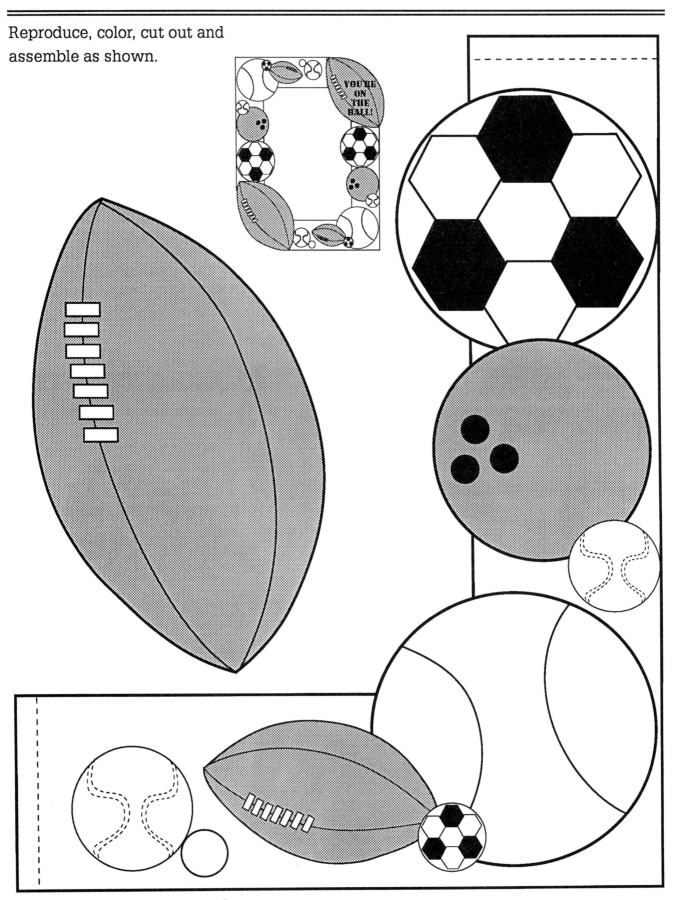

YOU'RE ON THE BALL!

Beehive

Reproduce, color, cut out and
assemble as shown.

Beehive

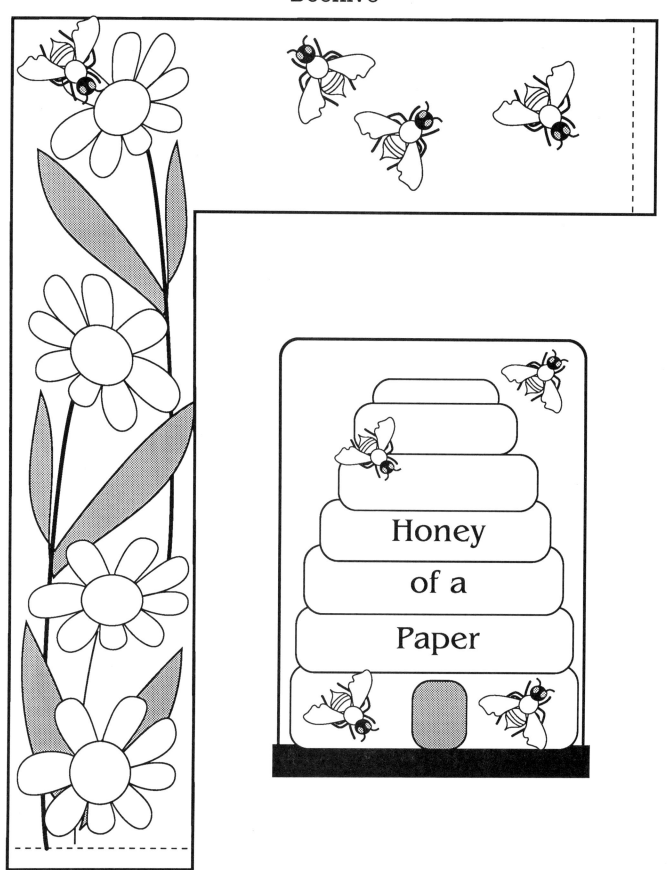

Honey

of a

Paper

Bird in Flight

Reproduce, color, cut out and assemble as shown.

You're Soaring High!

Bunny Rabbit

Reproduce, color, cut out and assemble as shown.

Hopping
Good
Work

Christmas Tree

Reproduce, color, cut out and assemble as shown. For a decorative bulletin board border, reduce and copy the tree design in two shades of green, repeating the design around edges of the board.

'Tis the Season to do Jolly Good Work!

Christmas Tree

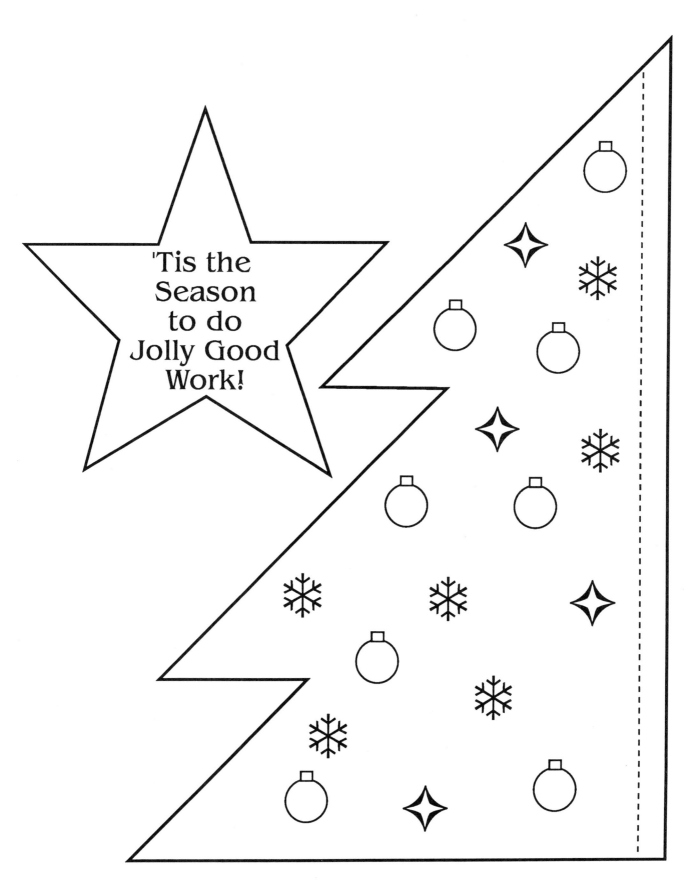

'Tis the
Season
to do
Jolly Good
Work!

Clown

Reproduce, color, cut out and assemble as shown.

Good Work Makes Me Giggle!

Cowboy/Cowgirl

Reproduce, color, cut out and assemble as shown. Cut off the pony tail to change the cowgirl to a cowboy.

I'm
Proud of
You, Partner!

Dinosaur

Reproduce, color, cut out and assemble as shown.

Best Work I've Seen In A Long Time

Dinosaur

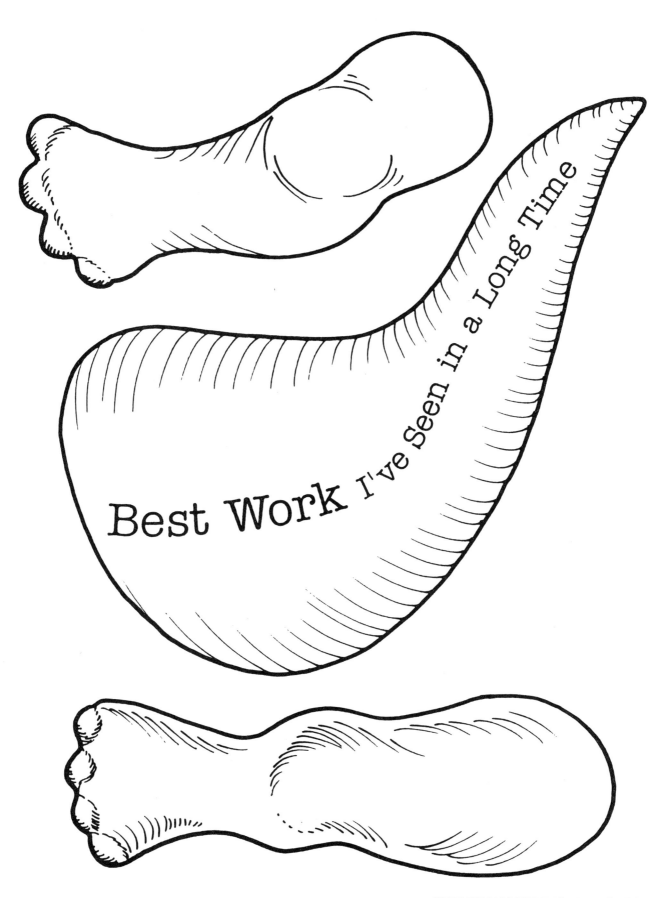

Best Work I've Seen in a Long Time

Drum Major

Reproduce, color, cut out and
assemble as shown.

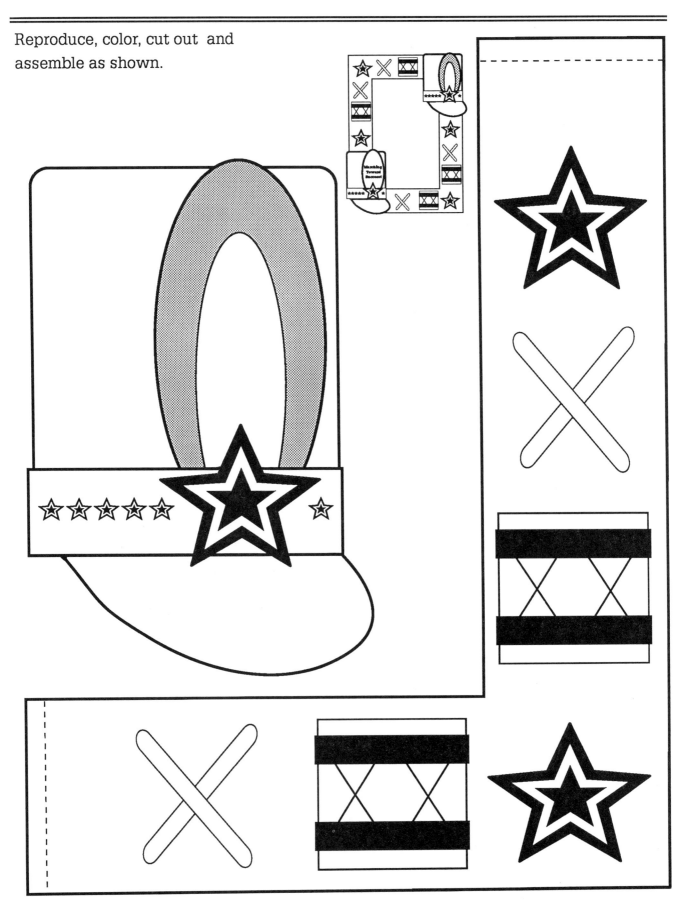

Drum Major

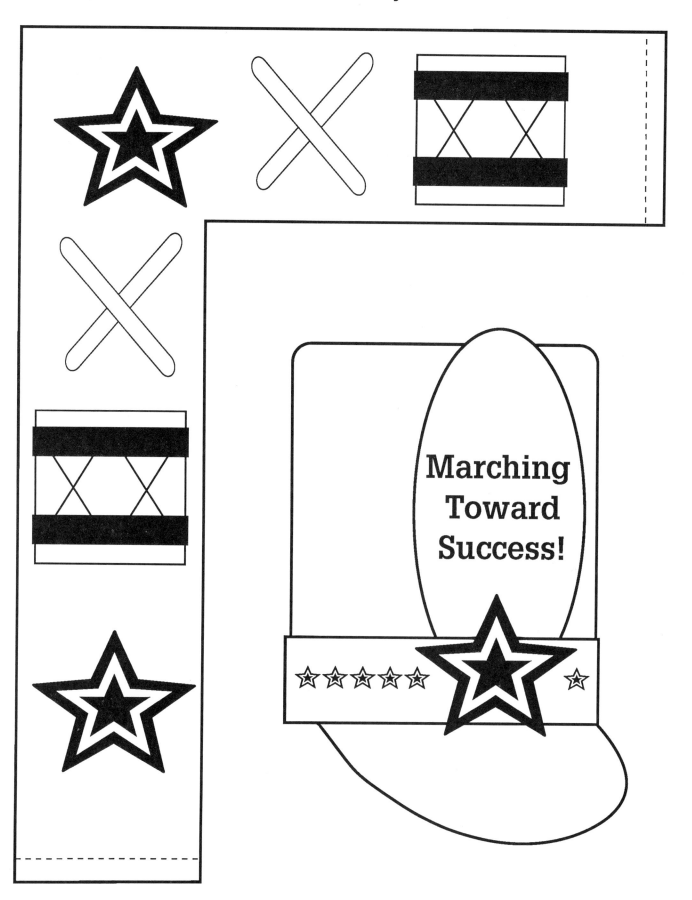

Marching Toward Success!

Fairy Tale

Reproduce, color, cut out and assemble as shown.

You're
Climbing
High!

Fairy Tale

George Washington

Reproduce, color, cut out and assemble as shown.

I cannot
tell a lie...

George Washington

You're GREAT!

Solar System

Reproduce, color, cut out and assemble as shown.

Solar System

Leprechaun and Shamrocks

Reproduce, color, cut out and assemble as shown.

Work this Nice
Takes
More than Luck!

Leprechaun and Shamrocks

Mountain Climber

Reproduce, color, cut out and assemble as shown.

Mountain Climber

Pelican

Reproduce, color, cut out and assemble as shown.

I'm Proud
as a Pelican!
I Did My Best!

Pelican

Pencil and Sharpener

Reproduce, color, cut out and assemble as shown.

You're
Looking
Sharp!

You're
Looking
Sharp!

Notes

Pencil and Sharpener

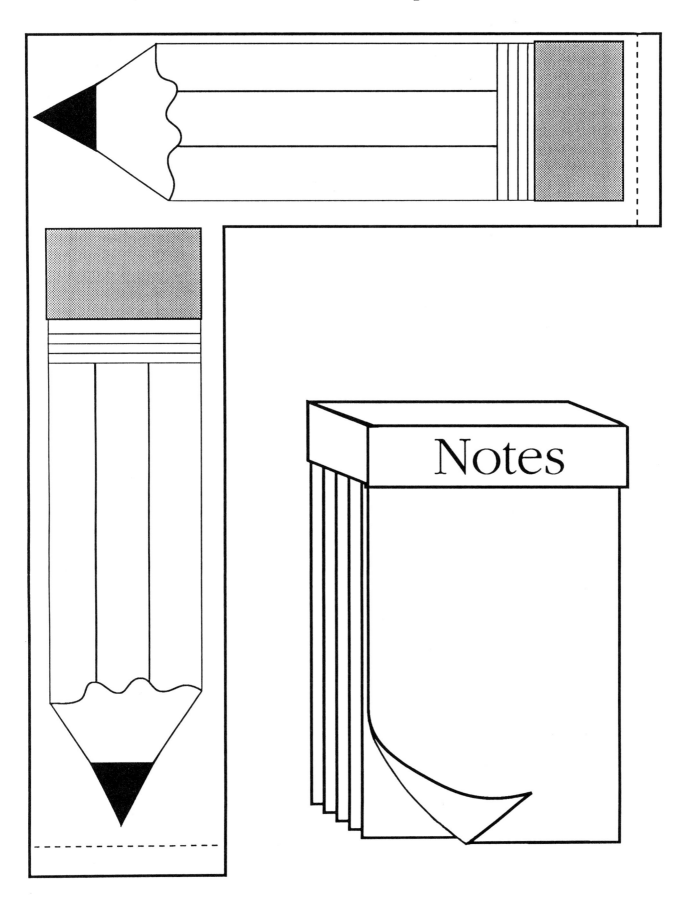

Notes

Chef's Pots and Pans

Reproduce, color, cut out and assemble as shown.

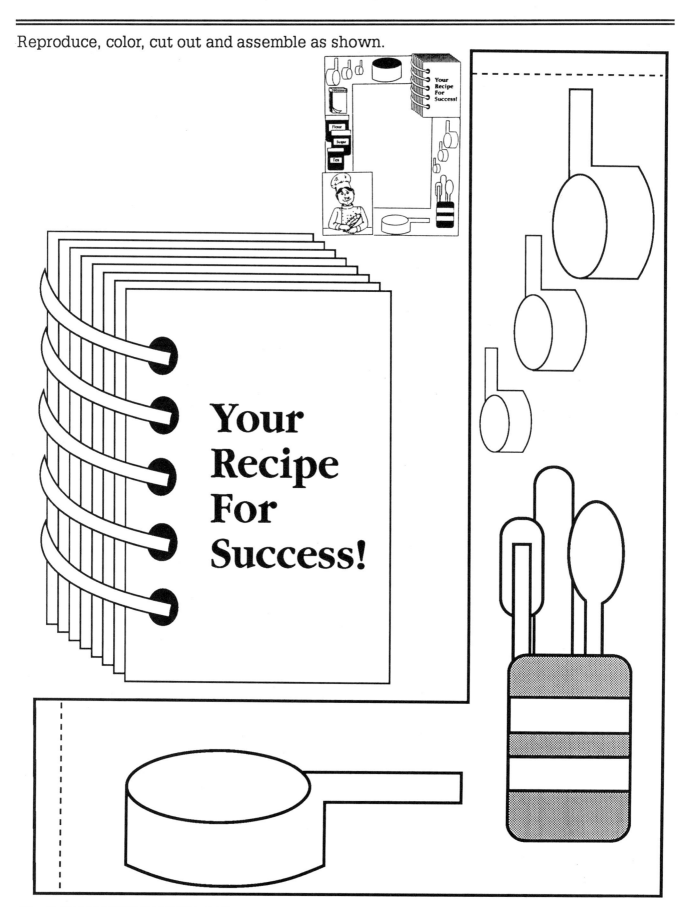

Your Recipe For Success!

Chef's Pots and Pans

Groceries

Flour

Sugar

Tea

Pumpkin Patch

Reproduce, color, cut out and assemble as shown.

Your Work Is Purrfectly
Bewitching!

Pumpkin Patch

Rock Group

Reproduce, color, cut out and assemble as shown.

Now You're Rockin'!

Rock Group

Santa Claus

Reproduce, color, cut out and assemble as shown.

Santa Claus

Ship

Reproduce, color, cut out and assemble as shown.

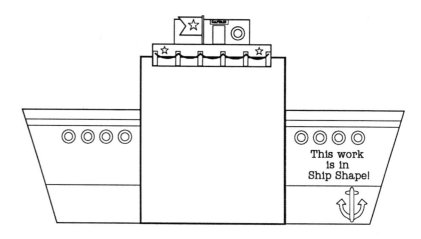

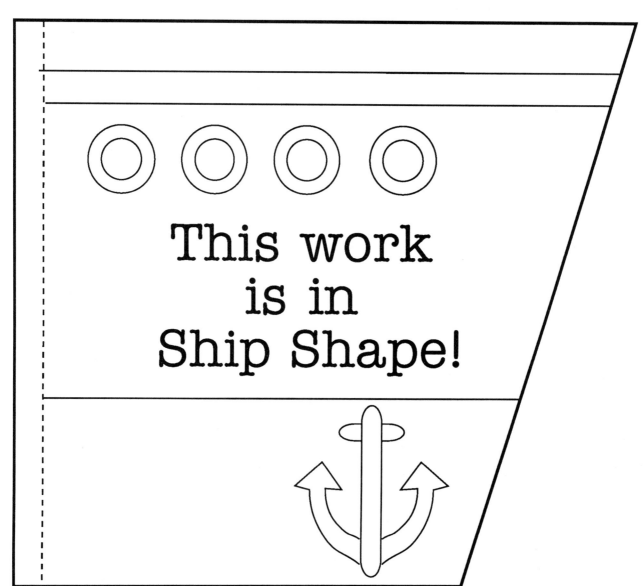

Ship

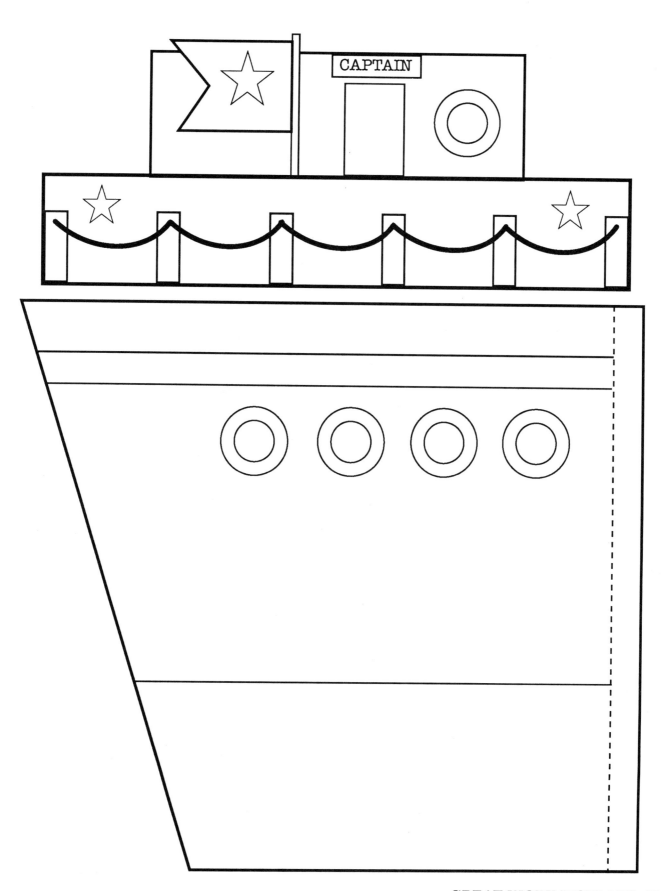

Seal

Reproduce, color, cut out and assemble as shown. Fold a 6" piece of ribbon in half and glue it under the medallion for a fancier look.

Space Shuttle

Reproduce, color, cut out and assemble as shown.

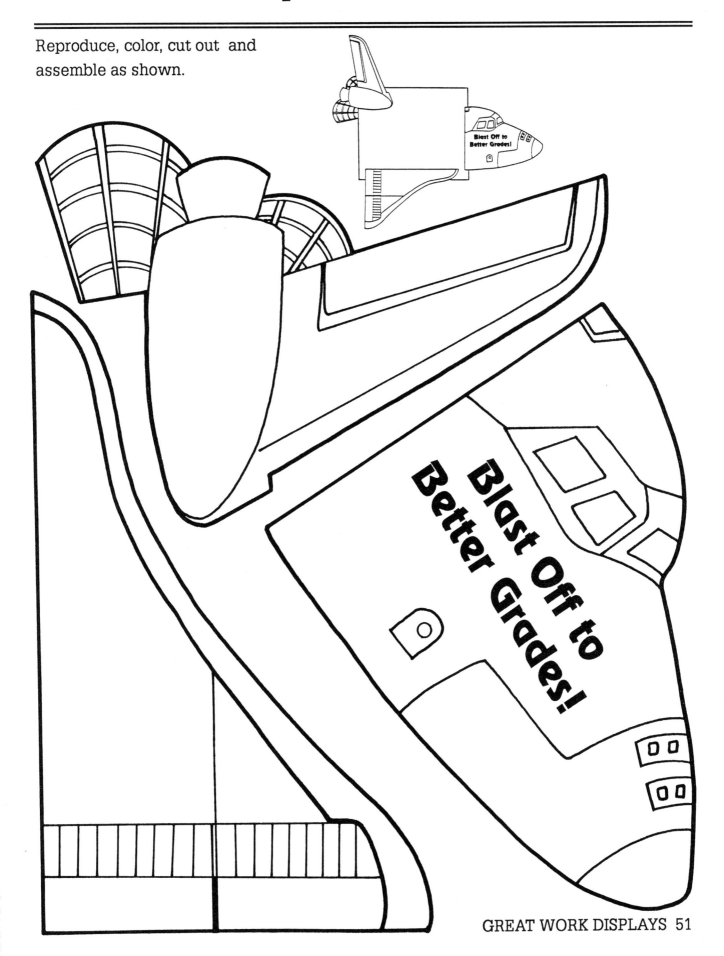

Blast Off to Better Grades!

Snowy Day

Reproduce, color, cut out and assemble as shown.

Snowy Day

Baseball Bear

Reproduce, color, cut out and assemble as shown.

You're Batting a Thousand!

Baseball Bear

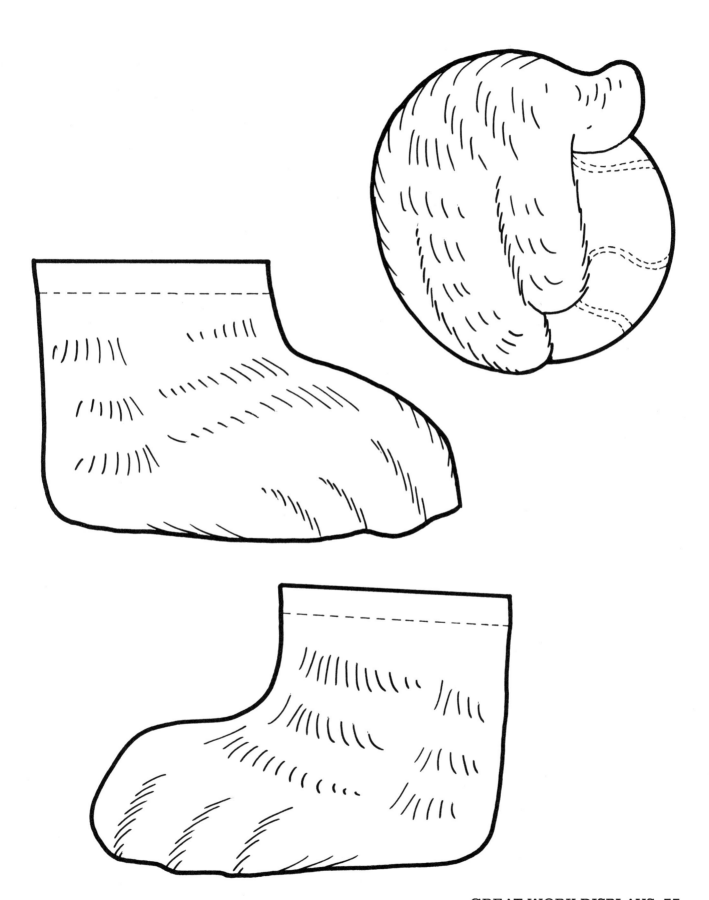

Tiger

Reproduce, color, cut out and assemble as shown.

Toucan

Reproduce, color, cut out and assemble as shown.

You Toucan Do Good Work!

Turkey

Reproduce, color, cut out and assemble as shown.

I'm Struttin' My Stuff!

I'm Struttin' My Stuff!

Valentine

Reproduce, color, cut out
and assemble as shown.

I Love
to Do My
Best!

Valentine

Witch

Reproduce, color, cut out
and assemble as shown.

This is So Good...

Ant Hair

Recipes

Potions

Witch

Bug Ears

Spells, Etc.

Magic

It's SCARY!

Whiz Kid

Reproduce, color, cut out and assemble as shown. Attach the bow for a girl.

I'm a
Whiz Kid!

Chapter 2: Goal Achievers

Goal achievers help children see how they are progressing one step at a time toward set goals. Tell the class what they will be learning and show them each step that must be taken to reach the goal. When a step is completed, reward the class or individual with one of the achiever emblems.

You can link them across a bulletin board to measure class progress or string them on yarn for individual achievements to make a bracelet, necklace or desk decoration. Collecting the pieces helps children see that goals are reached one step at a time and that progressing in proper order helps them learn more easily. Reward a student with a certificate or award from Chapter 4 when a set number of pieces has been earned.

Reaching Goals

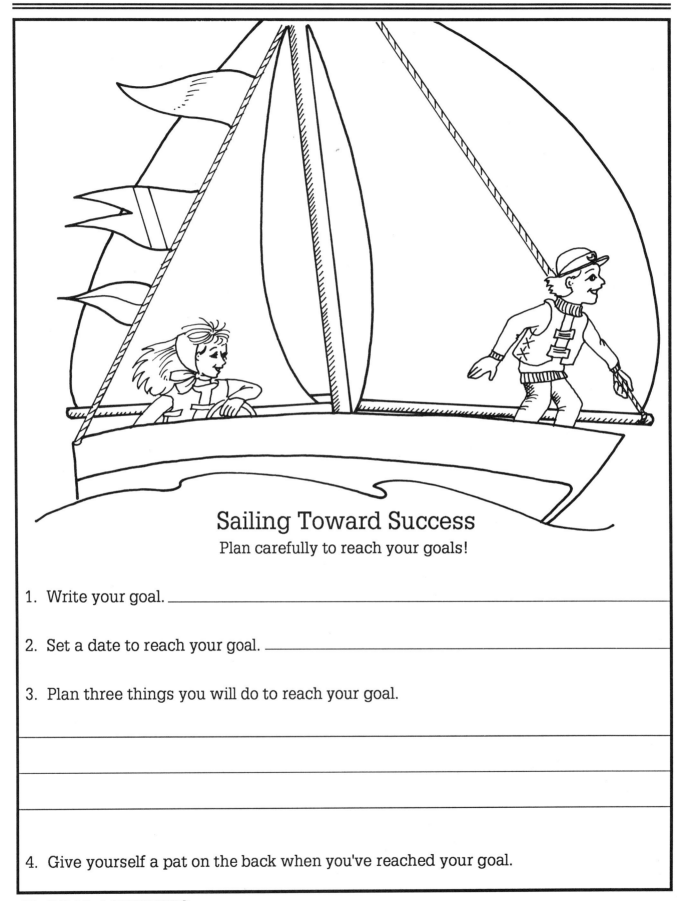

Sailing Toward Success
Plan carefully to reach your goals!

1. Write your goal. _____

2. Set a date to reach your goal. _____

3. Plan three things you will do to reach your goal.

_____

_____

_____

4. Give yourself a pat on the back when you've reached your goal.

123 Math Building Cards

Reproduce the cards, mount on sturdy tagboard, cut out and cut slits on black lines. Write math facts or practice problems on the back of each card. As children master the problems, they can build towers by sticking the cards together on the slits.

ABC's Compliments Chain

Reproduce, cut out and color the strips. Glue them into chains to create garlands of good news and praise.

Your work is **A**LWAYS on time. Good Job!

You're doing **B**ETTER. Keep it up!

I like your **C**URIOSITY.

This project has nice **D**ETAILS. Good work!

You got **E**VERY answer correct!

This is **F**INE work.

You did a **G**REAT job on this paper.

I appreciate your **H**ELPFULNESS.

ABC's Compliments Chain

Wow! What an **I**MAGINATION!

Try **J**UST a little harder. You're making good progress!

Your **K**INDNESS to others makes this room a happier place.

You are always ready to **L**EARN. I like being your teacher.

I like your good **M**ANNERS.

This paper is very **N**EAT.

You have a very **O**RGANIZED desk.

I like the way you always **P**ARTICIPATE in class.

You ask good **Q**UESTIONS. It helps us all to learn!

ABC's Compliments Chain

You **R**EAD that whole book. Good job!

You **S**PELLED all the words right!

I like the way you always **T**RY to do things.

I appreciate the way you **U**NDERSTAND other children's feelings.

You did a **V**ERY nice job with this.

WOW, what a **W**ONDERFUL score!

Keep up the good work and someday you'll be an E**X**PERT.

YIPPEE! **Y**OU did it!

Your good spirits bring **Z**EST to our classroom!

Artist's Paint Box

Reproduce for each child. Color in a space on the paint box each time a goal is reached.

Cowboy/Cowgirl Dress 'Ems

Dress 'em up, cowpokes! Reproduce, color and mount child on tagboard. Cut off pony tail for a cowboy. Fold tabs to stand. Color, cut out and glue on appropriate clothes as they are earned.

Go-Get 'Em Galaxy Charms

Reproduce these planetary platitudes, color and cut out as needed. Punch holes and string on lengths of yarn to hang, wear, or place on a classroom mobile.

Musical Message Puzzle

Reproduce, cut out, color, glue charms in place and and put strips together in order to see a musical message!

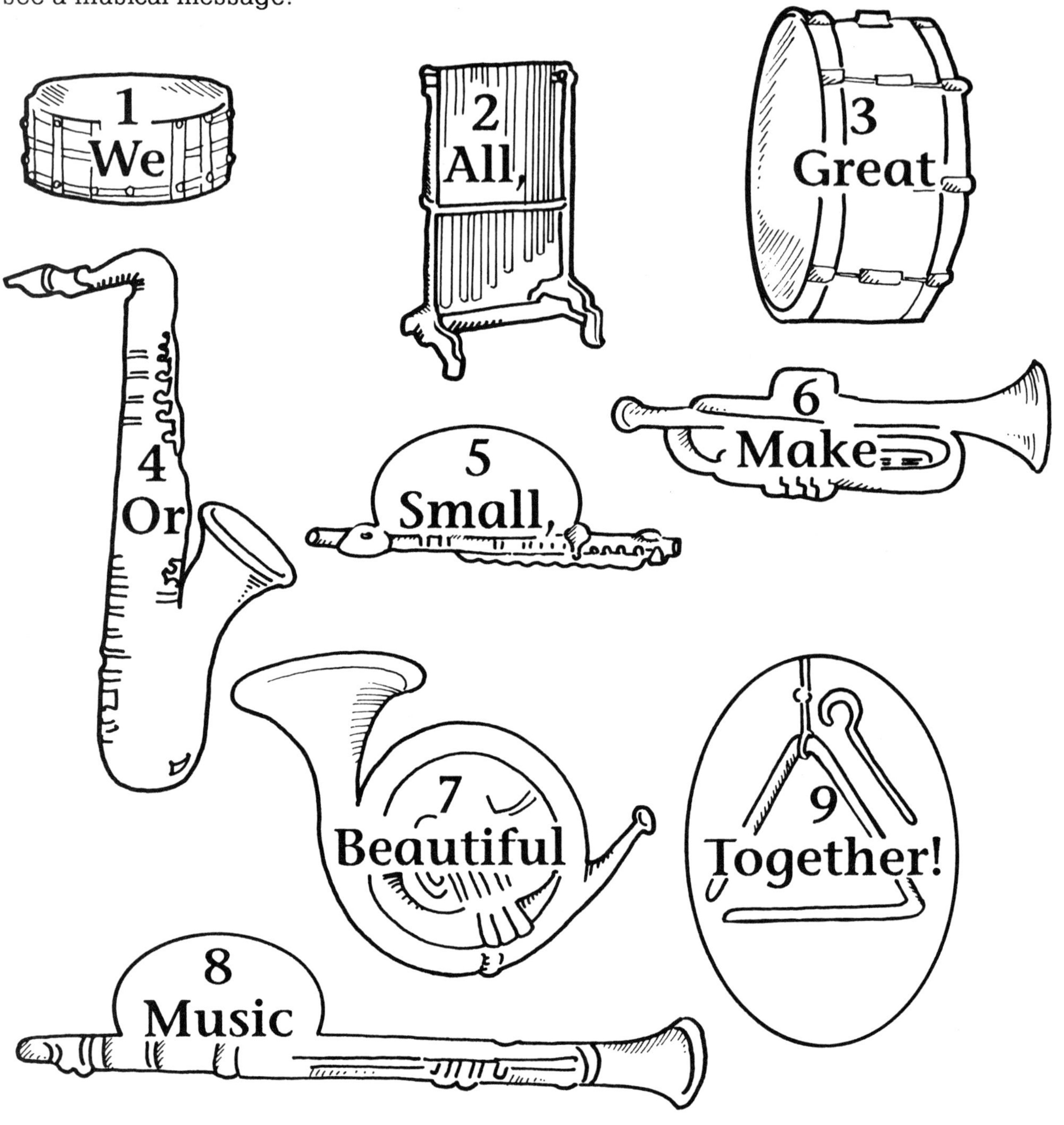

1
We
2
All,
3
Great
4
Or
5
Small,
6
Make
7
Beautiful
8
Music
9
Together!

1
We
2
All
3
Great
4
Or
5
Small,
6
Make
7
Beautiful
8
Music
9
Together!

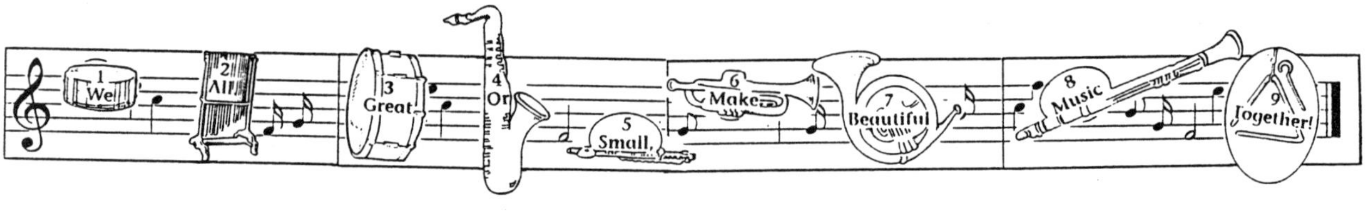

Musical Message Puzzle

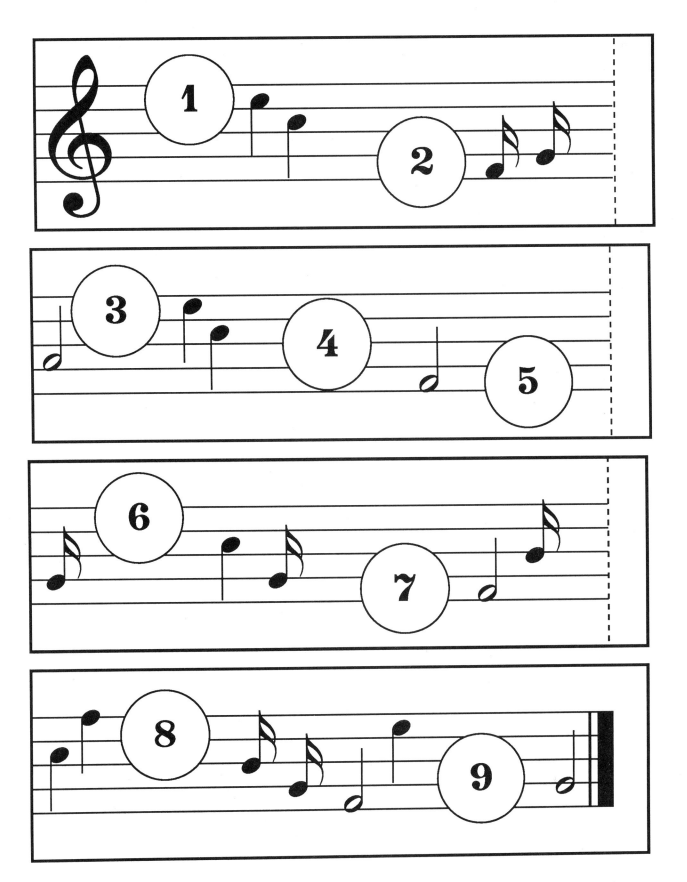

Good Sports Bag and Charms

Drawstring gym bags made from brown paper lunch bags will store sporty slogans to cut out and color.

Materials Needed:
1 brown lunch bag per child
Crayons
24" yarn or curling ribbon per child
Glue

Directions:

- Decorate the bag with initials or a favorite sports motif three inches below the top of the bag.
- Fold top of bag down 3 " along outside of bag.
- Cut one small hole in top folded edge.
- Place yarn or curling ribbon under the fold and pull ends out of hole.
- Glue bottom of folded edge to bag to create a casing. (Do not glue ribbon!)
- When dry, gently pull ribbon and tie in a bow to close top of bag.
- Reproduce, color and cut out sports charms. Collect them in the bags.

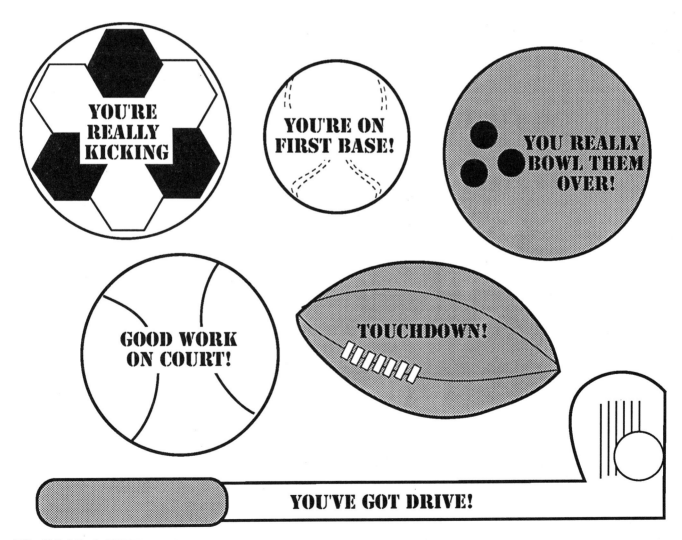

Elephant Links

Copy, cut out, color and link these praising pachyderms to parade across desks or bulletin boards.

Elephants never forget...
Neither did you!
Good Work!

_____
name

Elephants never forget...
Neither did you!
Good Work!

_____
name

Get up and Grow! Pencil Holder

Practical praises with color and cut out accents make great desk toppers or gifts.

Materials Needed:

Garden fence and flower reproducible

Clean, dry 14 oz. soup can (1 per child)

Scissors

Crayons

Tape or glue

Directions:

- Copy a fence for each child.
- Cut out, color and tape around soup can.
- Cut out flowers as earned and add to the garden to decorate.

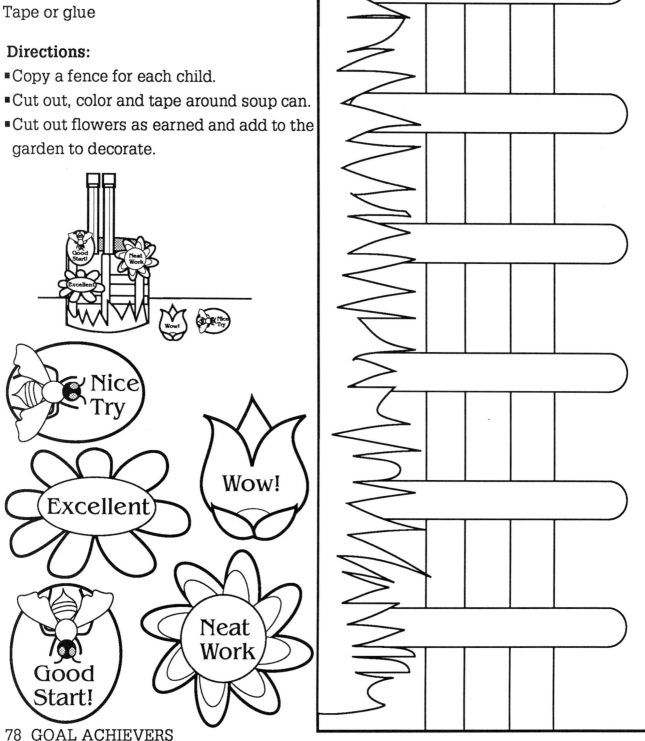

Seashell Praises Pencil Holder

More praises with reproducible color and cut out accents to create desk toppers or gifts.

Materials:

Seashore and shells reproducible

Clean, dry 14 oz. soup can (1 per child)

Scissors

Crayons

Tape or glue

Directions:

- Copy a shore for each child.
- Cut out, color and tape around soup can.
- Cut out shells as earned and add to the shore to decorate.

Circus Train Links

Reproduce, color and cut out. Send a circus train chugging across desks or bulletin boards by linking them together.

We'll do Flips
for Work this Good!
Thanks,_____
(name)

You Made a Great Start...
_____
(name)

Circus Train Links

You Gave it a Big Top Try!
Keep up the Good Work!

_____
(name)

You're Making Progress!
Keep Chugging Along!

_____
(name)

Cornucopia Charms

Bountiful praises for the classroom! Reproduce, color and cut out. Punch holes and string onto yarn to wear or enlarge to use on a bulletin board.

See the fruits of my labors!

Cornucopia Charms

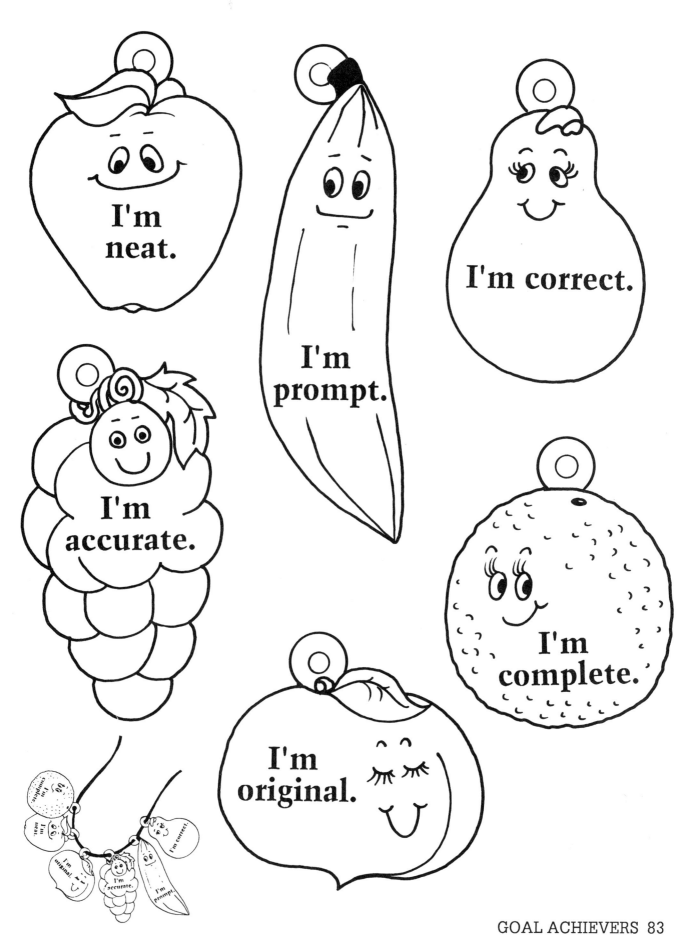

Dinosaur Links

Mesozoic titans for desks or bulletin boards! Reproduce, color, cut out and link together.

You're never too big to learn!

Easter Basket

Reproduce, color and cut out baskets that will be brimming with good news.

Materials:

Easter basket reproducible (1 per child)

Handful of Easter grass per child or 1/2
    sheet of green tissue paper

Scissors

Glue

Crayons

Directions:

- Copy a basket for each child.
- Glue Easter grass or crumpled green tissue paper on top of the basket. Let dry.
- Proudly tuck the eggs into the basket as they are earned!

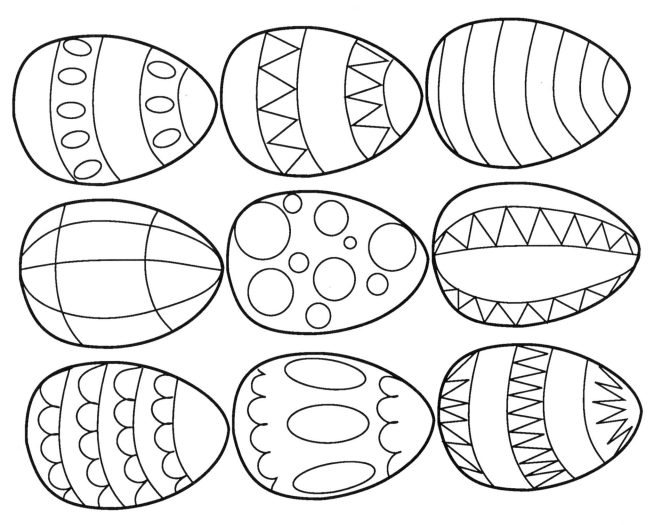

Easter Basket

"Eggs"ellent Work!

Souped Up Students

Copy, cut out and string onto yarn for an unusual necklace or make into a classroom bulletin board.

Souped Up For Study!

Souped Up Students

HAPPY

CURIOUS

THINKING

LISTENING

BRIGHT

EAGER

READY

INTERESTED

Fairy Tale Bookmarks

Complimentary bookmarks to reproduce, cut out and color

Your imagination is like a magic castle full of adventures!

Your work is of imperial quality!

Your behavior is pure gold!

Fairy Tale Bookmarks

Baubles and Beads

Reproduce, cut out and color. Punch holes and string onto yarn to wear this friendly finery.

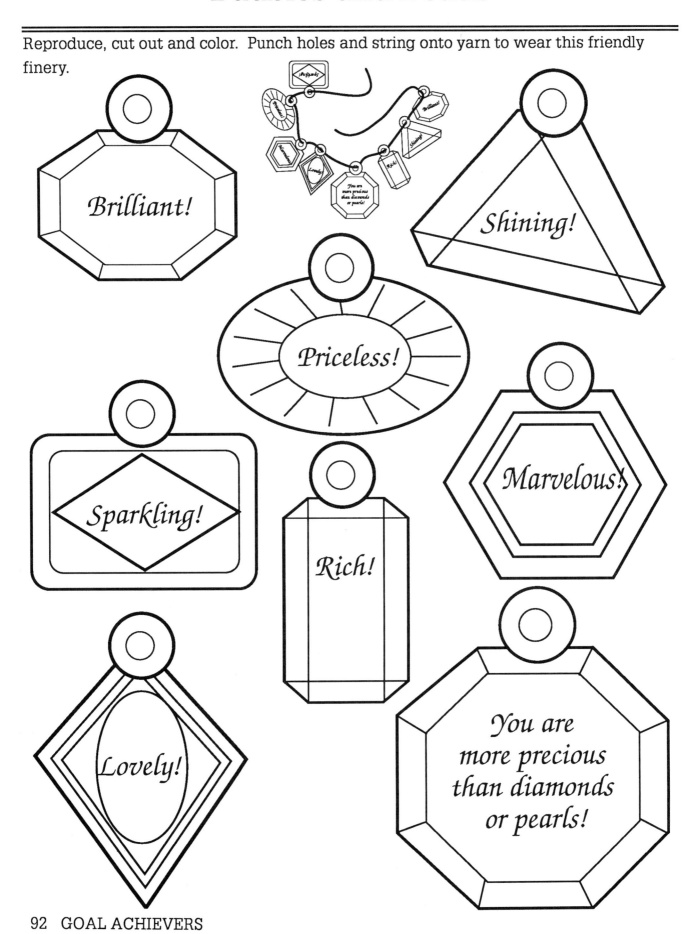

Shipmates' Flags

Reproduce, cut out and color the flags. String on desks or add to the ship display from Chapter 1.

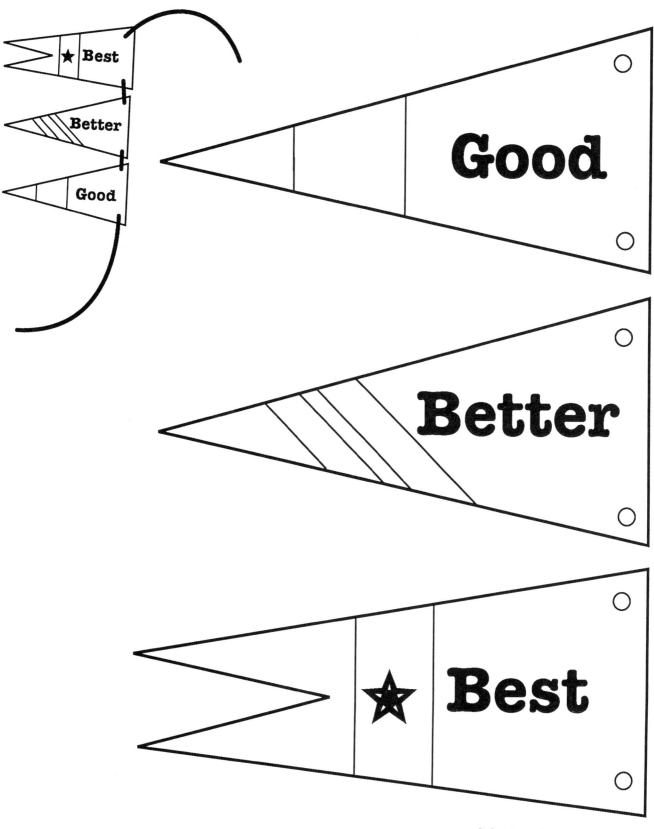

Jungle Charms

String oodles of zoo friends onto yarn or use on a bulletin board.

Kangaroo Desk Topper

A "hopping good" project to reproduce, color, cut out and assemble

Directions:
- Reproduce on heavy tagboard.
- Cut out kangaroo and joey.
- Cut slits and fold along dotted lines.
- Tape or glue to secure.
- Tuck joey in flap.

Hopping
Good
Work!

_____
(name)

FOLD FORWARD

FOLD BACK

FOLD BACK

Sharing Time: Improving Myself

Reproduce. Talk about ways children can improve work habits or behavior. Fill in strategies.

I CAN DO BETTER IF I...

Write down what you need to improve.

_____

_____

_____

_____

_____

Write ideas of how to do it.

_____

_____

_____

_____

_____

Sharing Time: Self-Awareness

Reproduce. Talk about special talents and strengths. Identify them.

Mountain Mottos

Good study habits to reproduce, color, cut and paste

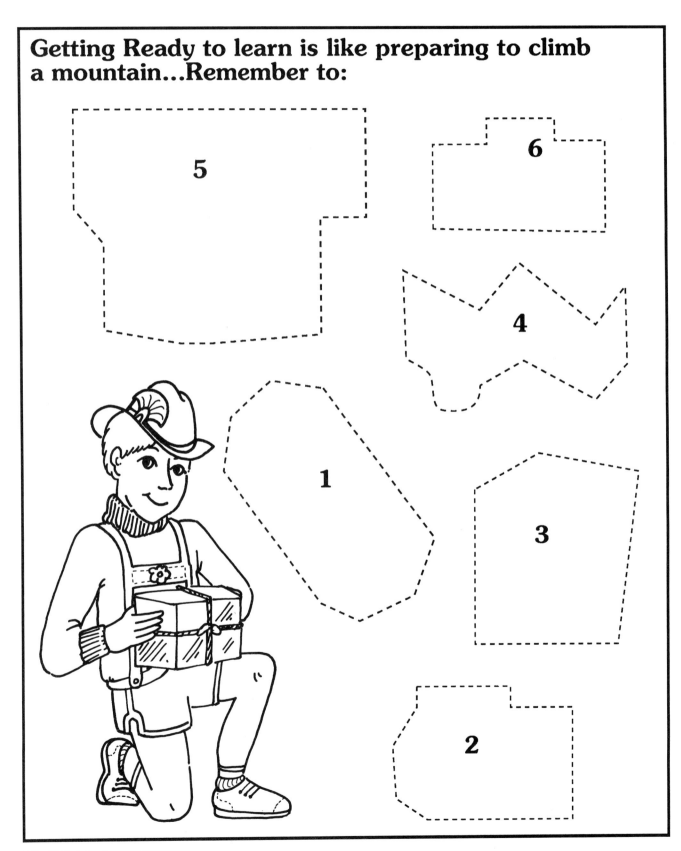

Getting Ready to learn is like preparing to climb a mountain...Remember to:

5

6

4

1

3

2

Mountain Mottos

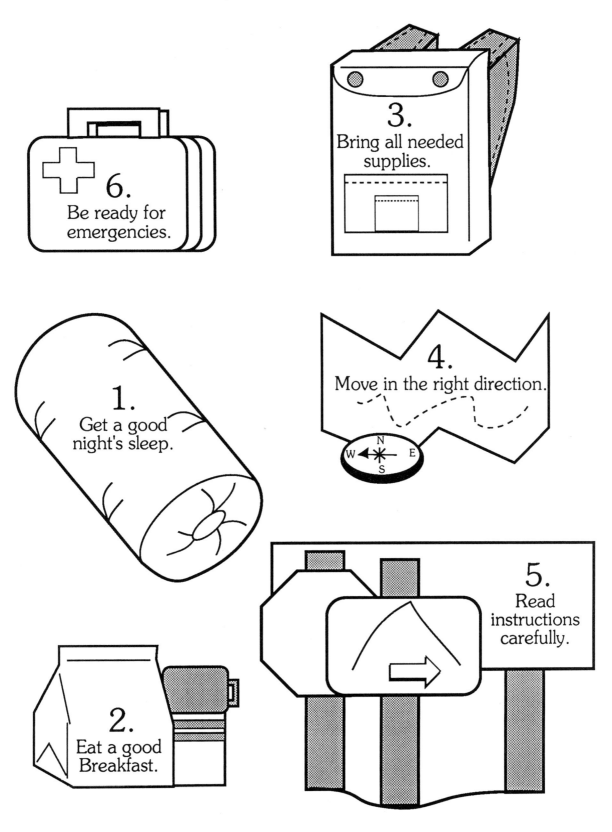

6. Be ready for emergencies.

3. Bring all needed supplies.

1. Get a good night's sleep.

4. Move in the right direction.

5. Read instructions carefully.

2. Eat a good Breakfast.

Fairy Tale Goal Setter

Reproduce. Talk about plans and dreams. Write some on the leaves.

Sharing Time: Friendship

Reproduce. Talk and write about friendship. What do friends like about each other?

Passport

Reproduce, cut out, collate and staple in the middle to assemble. Make one book for each child. Establish goals and reward with passport stamps to color, cut out and paste in the passport book.

Passport Cover: Copy one per child on colored paper.

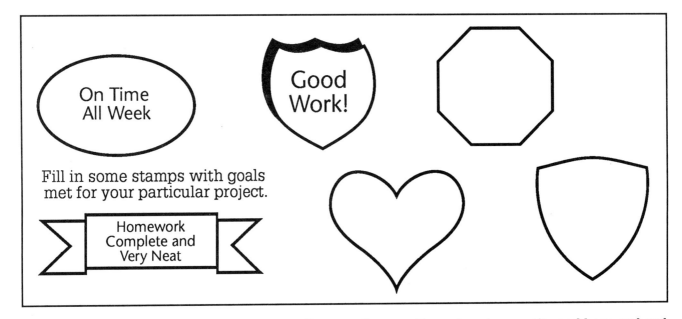

Passport Stamps: Reproduce in quantity and have on hand.

PASSPORT for Great Achievers

I hereby pledge to try my best to achieve my goals.

_____

Student's Signature   Date

Student's Name

School   Grade

Paste student photo here.

I certify that this is an offical school achievement PASSPORT and that I will do whatever I can to help the bearer plan and achieve his or her goals.

_____

Teacher Signature

If this passport is found, please return it to the owner immediately.

Inside Cover: Copy one per book. Print on or glue inside cover.

Goal:_____

Class or Subject: _____

Place official stamps or stickers here for achievement.

Goal: _____

Class or Subject: _____

Place official stamps or stickers here for achievement.

It is the responsibility of the PASSPORT owner to do his or her own work.

Inside Pages: Copy one or more on white paper.

Pelican's Best Qualities

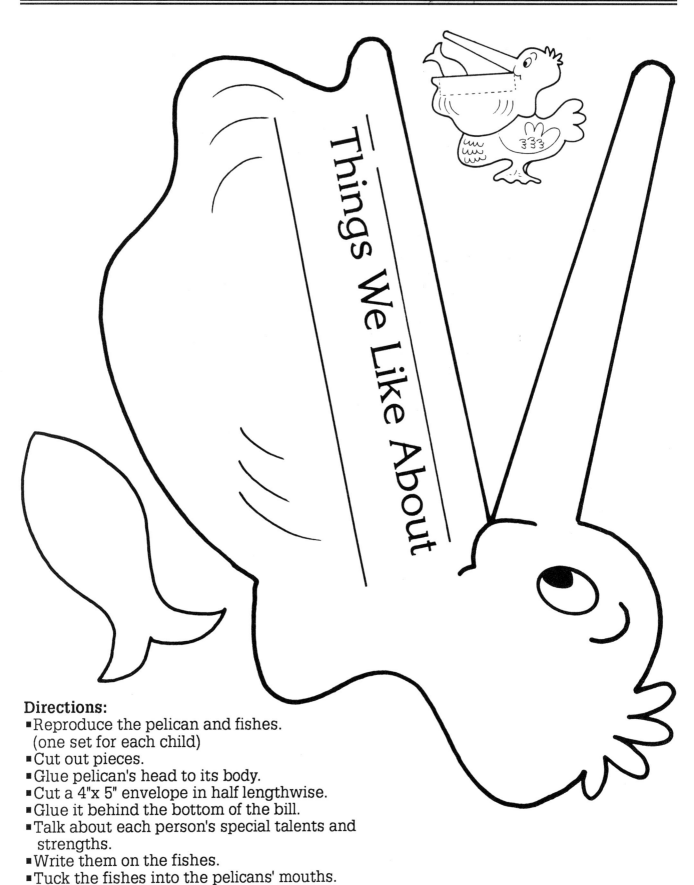

Things We Like About

Directions:
- Reproduce the pelican and fishes.
  (one set for each child)
- Cut out pieces.
- Glue pelican's head to its body.
- Cut a 4"x 5" envelope in half lengthwise.
- Glue it behind the bottom of the bill.
- Talk about each person's special talents and
  strengths.
- Write them on the fishes.
- Tuck the fishes into the pelicans' mouths.

Pelican's Best Qualities

Pats and Praises Pencil Toppers

Holiday characters to reproduce, color, cut out, punch and perch on pencil tops

More Pencil Toppers

Use these pencil toppers with other themes in the book. Reproduce, color, cut out, punch and perch on pencils.

Gold Medals and Blue Ribbons

Don't let a good job go unnoticed. Reproduce, color, cut out and keep on hand for generous praise. Add your own messages to the center of each.

Pats and Praises Rebus I

Puzzle-full praises for special days

TH+

R

GRRR

+8!

Signed,

_____

Answer: I think you are great!

Pats and Praises Rebus II

Puzzle-full praises for special days.

+P

the

G+   -W

-M + K.

Signed,

_____

Solution: Keep up the good work.

Rock Band Rocker Toy

Reproduce, color, cut out, assemble and rock and roll.

Directions:

- Color all pieces.
- Glue circle on tagboard. Cut out.
- Fold circle base in half.
- Cut out the rock band.
- Glue it onto base near fold.
- Tap lightly to get it rocking.

GLUE HERE

Now You're Rockin'!

Special Day Loom I

Children discover encouraging words when they earn all four strips and weave them into place.

Directions:
- Reproduce both patterns on different pastel colors of construction paper.
- Cut apart strips on this page and hand out as rewards.
- Fold loom base piece in half and cut along the heavy lines.
- Weave strips 1 and 3 over and under, strips 2 and 4 under and over through the base.

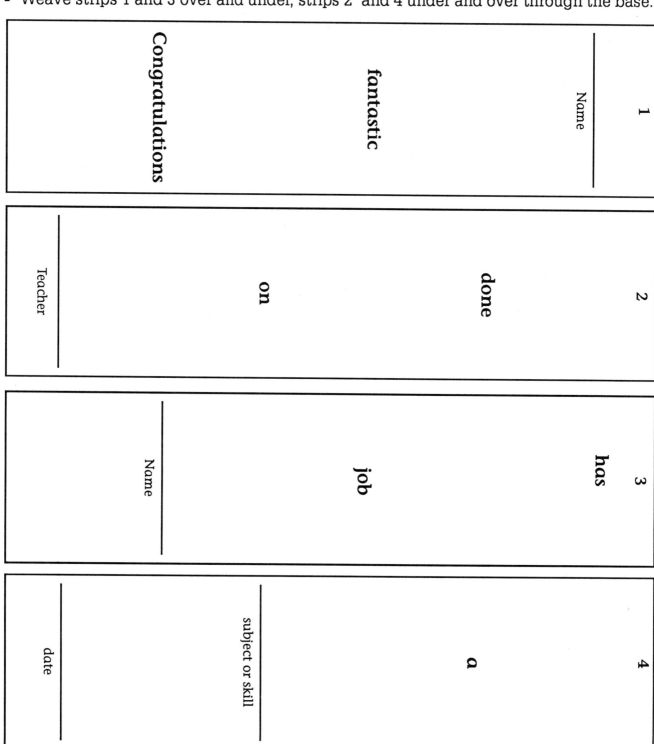

Special Day Loom I

1

2

3

4

Special Day Loom II

More encouraging messages in a craft activity.

Directions:
- Reproduce both patterns on different pastel colors of construction paper.
- Cut apart strips on this page and hand out as rewards.
- Fold base piece in half and cut along the heavy lines.
- Weave strips 1 and 3 over and under, 2 and 4 under and over through the base.

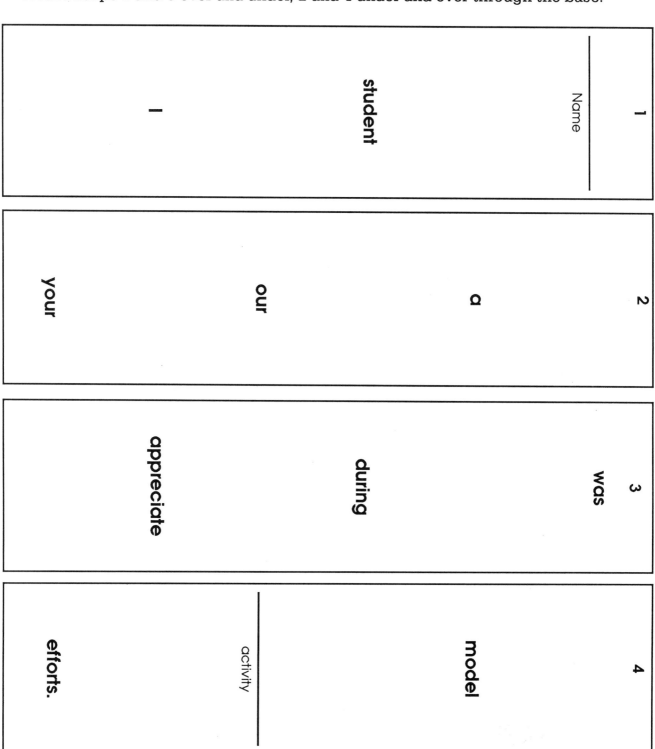

Special Day Loom II

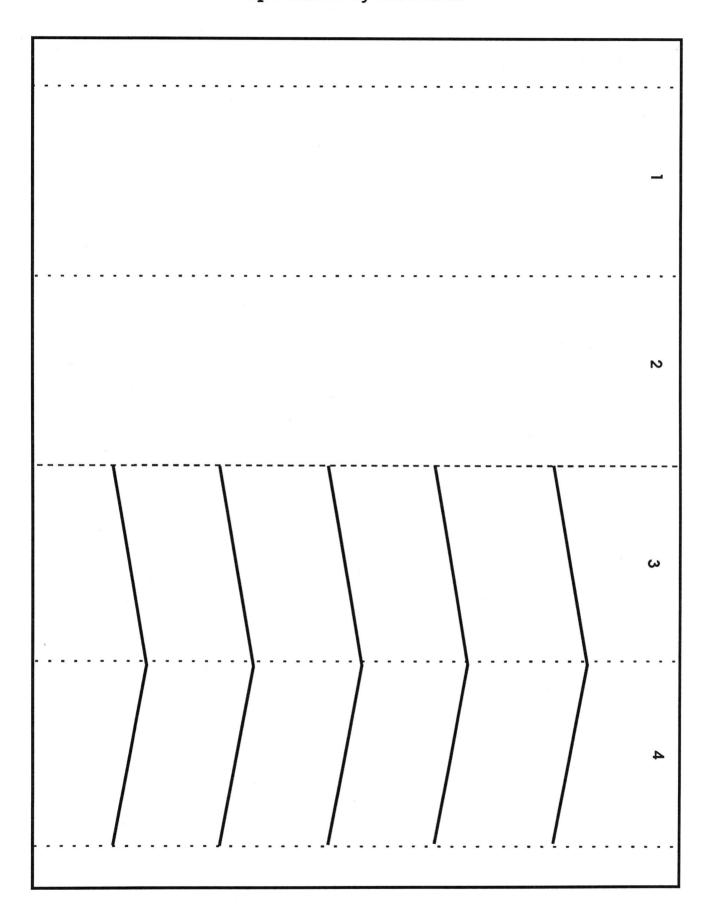

Special Day Loom III

Another compliment to earn and complete

Directions:
- Reproduce both patterns on different pastel colors of construction paper.
- Cut apart strips on this page and hand out as rewards.
- Fold base piece in half and cut along the heavy lines.
- Weave strips 1 and 3 over and under, strips 2 and 4 under and over through the base.

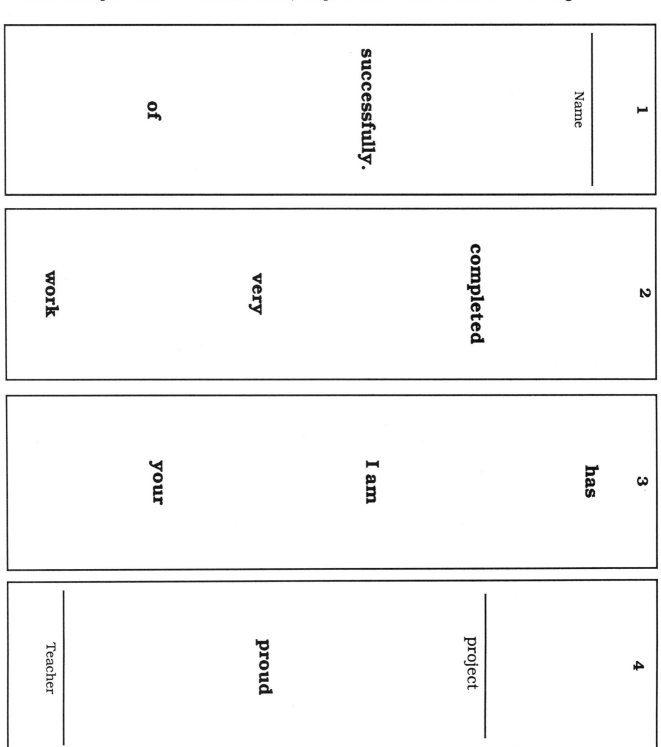

Special Day Loom III

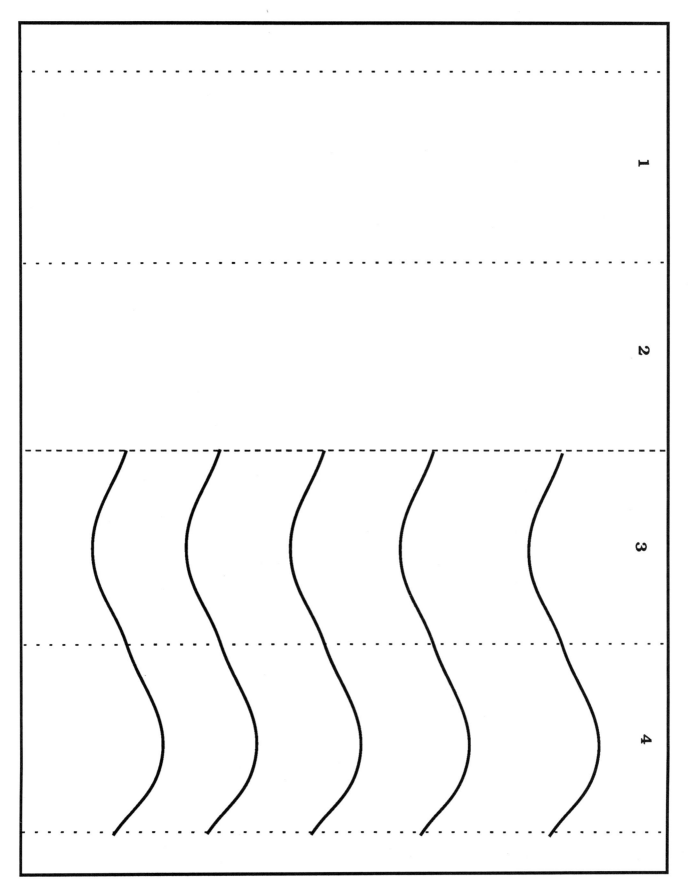

Pats and Praises Coupons

Students collect coupons for good behavior or for working toward goals. A handy folder holds them neatly.

Directions:

- Reproduce a coupon folder for each child.
- Cut out, fold, and glue flap to back.
- Reproduce lots of coupons.
- Fill in and award generously.

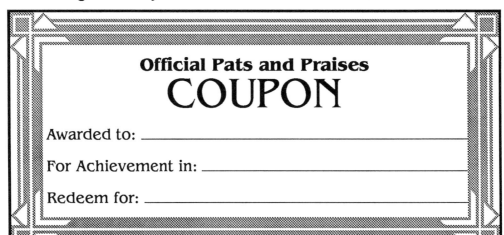

Pats and Praises Coupons

THIS OFFICIAL COUPON BOOK

BELONGS TO:

_____

Name

_____

School

Official Pats and Praises

COUPON SAVER

Snowman to Build

Reproduce these warm greetings for frosty fun. Complete the primary picture with snow man pieces earned for good school skills.

I RAISED MY HAND TO TALK

I WAS QUIET WHEN OTHERS SPOKE

I FINISHED MY WORK

I STAYED IN MY PLACE

I PAID ATTENTION

Rodeo Rockers

Reproduce, color, cut out, assemble and rock a bronco.

Directions:

- Color all pieces.
- Mount circle to tagboard. Cut out.
- Fold circle base in half.
- Cut out bronco and rider.
  Glue onto base near fold. Let dry.
- Tap lightly with finger to get it rocking.

GLUE HERE

Bronco Buster!

Bronco Buster!

Baseball Bear Links

For desks or bulletin boards!
Reproduce, color, cut out and link together.

Really Pitches in!

Catches on Quickly!

Sharing Time

A simple way to get to know your students.

Today Was a Great Day!

Draw some of the events that made it a good day.

Sharing Time

Let those feelings out!

Today Was Not My Day!

Draw what went wrong today.

Draw what you can do to make tomorrow better!

Sharing Time

Communication skills begin one-on-one. This easy format can help even shy students open up. Be sure to answer each letter! Use the home notes provided in Chapter 3.

Dear Teacher,

I was wondering if you _____.

My favorite part of class is when you _____.

Can we do more _____?

Why do we _____?

I _____ school. We _____ and _____.

Your student,

_____

Draw yourself here.

Responsibility

Howdy Partner! Are you ready to Learn?

Directions:
Cut off this strip.
Cut out pieces as earned and paste in place.

1. Put on your thinking hat!

2. Get to class on time!

3. Keep your questions on target!

4. Have your school supplies!

Chapter 3:
Home Notes

Home notes can be used as stationery for personal notes of praise for anything a child has done well at school. Keep several designs on hand for quick notes to the child or parent to let both know that you recognize that the child is improving in classroom behavior or subject areas.

Home notes can also encourage parents to get involved in coming events and study units at school. Use the notes as simple newletters or to request materials and parent assistance for any project you're planning. The notes can be sent home at regular intervals or whenever you need a little help. By gathering materials ahead of time, you'll have everything ready for that special program and parents will know what their child will be learning about ahead of time.

Home notes are also valuable for encouraging practice in skills-building. Use them as practice sheets for homework in any subject area. Just copy a page, add the homework assignment and duplicate enough pages for the class or group to take home to complete.

Reproduce for notes about math achievement or add math problems for a worksheet.

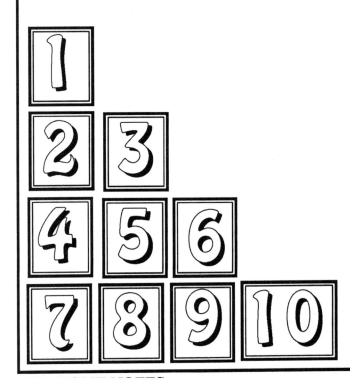

ABC's

Reproduce for handwriting practice, story writing or for any type of note.

A B C D E F G H I J K L M N O P

Z Y X W V U T S R Q

Artist's Easel

Reproduce for drawing practice or for a notice about an art exhibit or project.

Sports

Use for a note to a hard-working sports enthusiast or to announce a sports event.

 YOU'RE A GREAT SPORT!

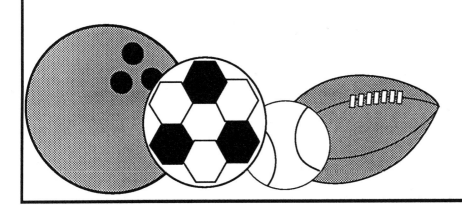

Music

Reproduce to announce a school concert, a note to a musically gifted student or for music assignments.

Bees and Flowers

 Happy! You're a  of a Kid!

Bunny

Use for any note or homework assignment.
Glue a cotton ball to the bunny's tail, if you like.

Hop to It!

Christmas Tree

Reproduce tree and cut out.

Write your note on the tree and add a star sticker at the top.

Lion Tamer

You can tame any wild assignment!

Clown

You're not just clowning around! You're learning!

Rodeo Round-Up Lasso Success!

You're a **Huge** Success!

GREAT WORK!

**You're like an elephant.
You never forget what you learn!**

★*Extra* Credit to You!★

You've Got a Wonderful Imagination.

Globe

From the World of _____ :

Whiz Kid Assignment Reminder

Students fill in this sheet to remind them of details for a special assignment or project.

Special Assignment

Title: _____

Due Date: _____

Directions: _____

_____

_____

References: _____

_____

Mountain Climber

You get to the top
one step at a time.

Open House

at _____ School

You're Invited!

Date: _____ **Time:** _____

You'll See: _____

_____

_____

Party Invitations

Use this sheet to invite parents to a class party or to request help with it.   If you're using these as an invitations only, just clip off the request for help.

We're Having a Party!

Party Theme:

Date:

Time:

Place:

We need your help.
Could you please bring:

We're Having a Party!

Party Theme:

Date:

Time:

Place:

We need your help.
Could you please bring:

Chef

Pelican

Take pride in your work!

Lost Tooth

Reproduce several of these to keep on hand for when a child loses a baby tooth at school. Tape the tooth in position for child to take home to the tooth fairy.

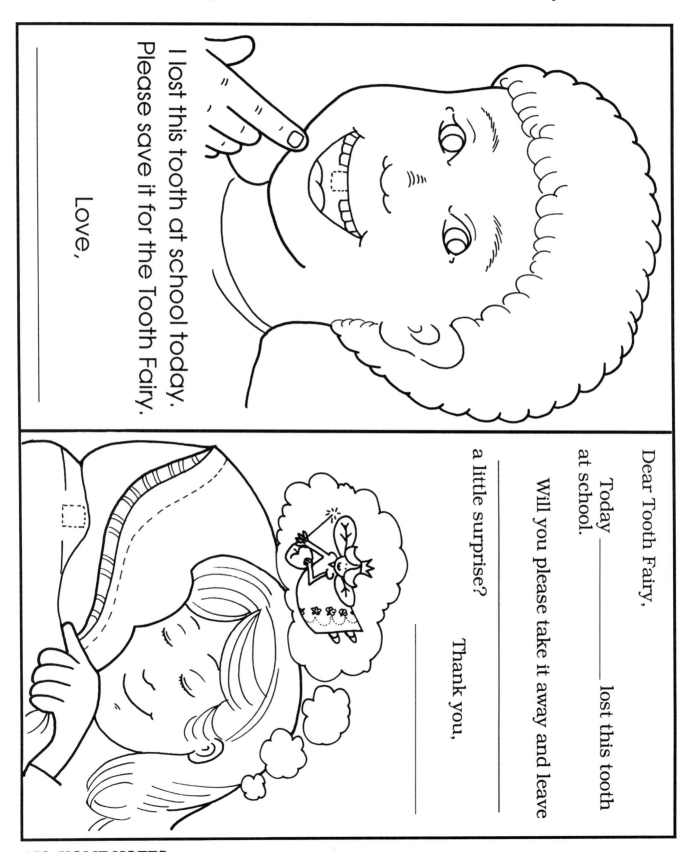

I lost this tooth at school today.
Please save it for the Tooth Fairy.

Love,

Dear Tooth Fairy,

Today _____ lost this tooth
at school.

Will you please take it away and leave

a little surprise?

Thank you,

You're a great kid!

Rock Drummer

 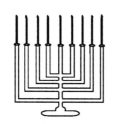  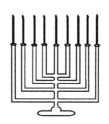 

Enjoy Your Holidays!

Sailing

You're sailing toward your highest goals.

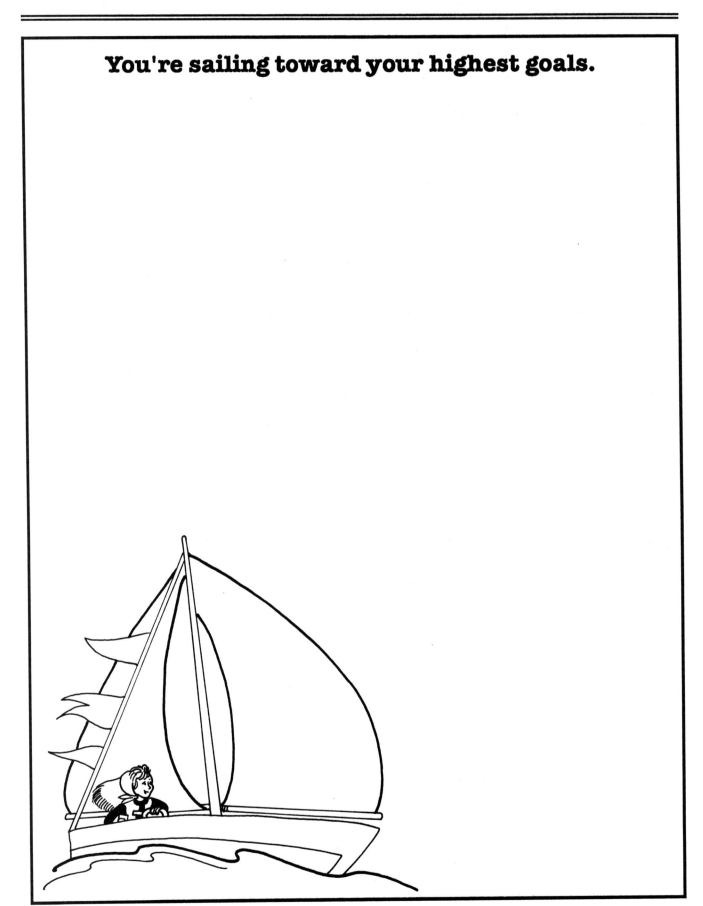

Space Shuttle

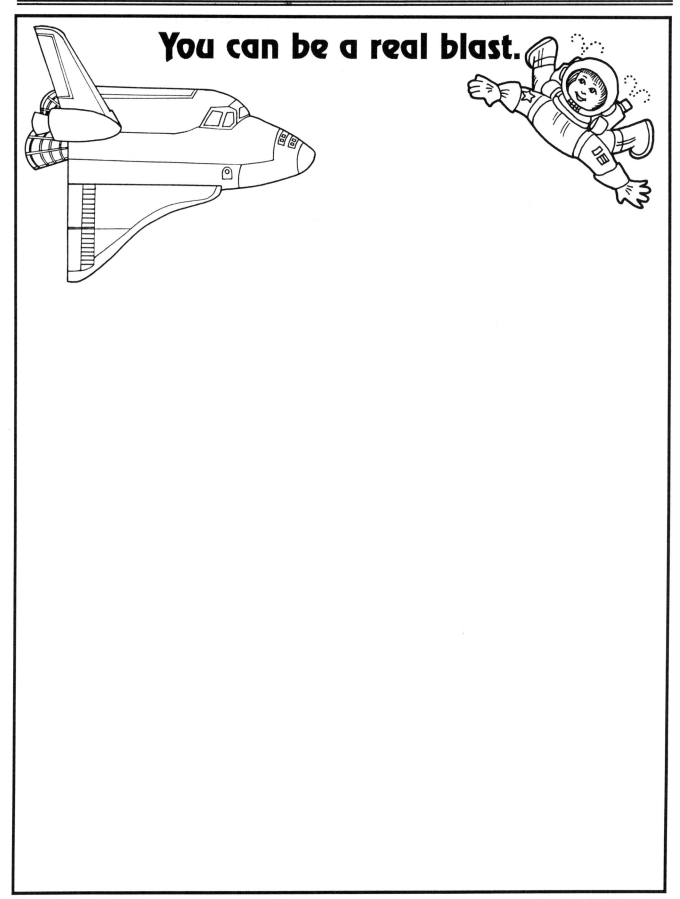

You can be a real blast.

Snowflakes

You're like a snowflake.
There's no one just like you.

Teacher

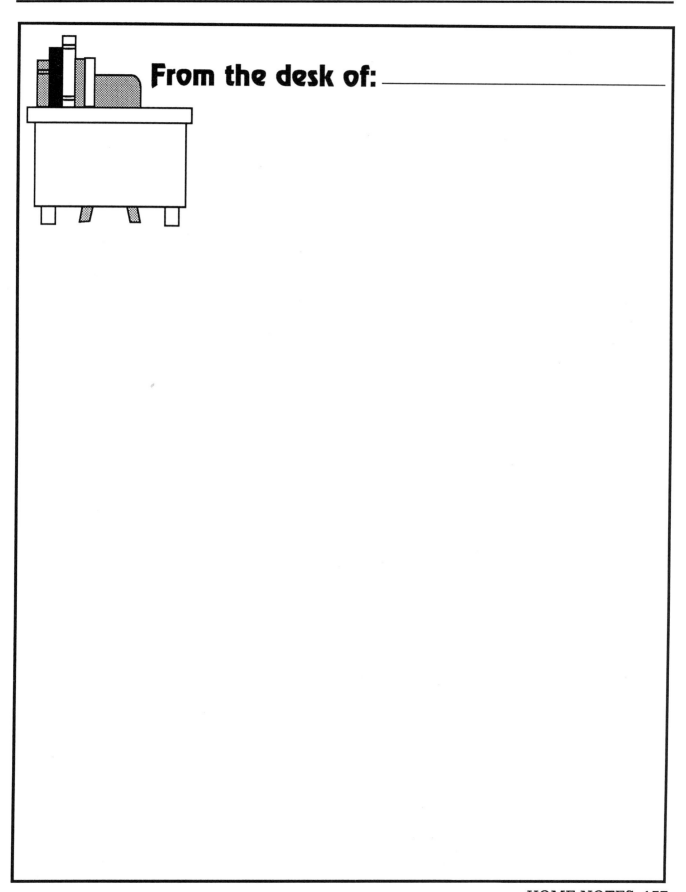

From the desk of: _____

Baseball Bear

Thank You

Thank You So Much

Toucan

You do a good job!

Turkey

Gobble, gobble,
good work!

Valentines

Let's get to the heart of the matter.

You're Great!

Ask Questions

Be Curious!

Imagine!

Keep Trying

Whiz Kid

Notes for Whiz Kids

Witch

You can stir up a great potion for success.

Chapter 4: Awards and Certificates

Awards help children feel a sense of accomplishment. This chapter has certificates of merit that the teacher gives a child or group of children working together when work is done. Some awards are simple cut and paste crafts the child can do when he or she has accomplished a specified task. Awards don't have to be earned over a long period. They can be given any time a child has earned your appreciation for a job well done.

Math

Use this certificate for any sort of math award.

For Achievement in Math

has really progressed in learning

Keep up the good work!

Signed

ABCs / Writing

Use for handwriting or any writing award.

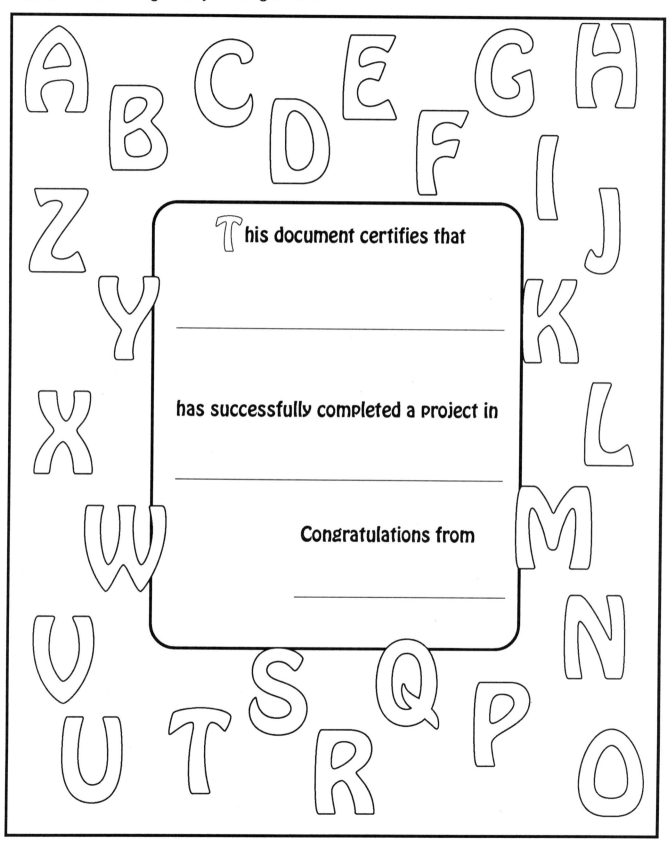

This document certifies that

_____

has successfully completed a project in

_____

Congratulations from

_____

Artist

Having completed a project in

_____

_____

has become a talented
artist in residence at

_____School

Signed _____

Batting a Thousand!

is scoring home runs in achievement of

Hip, Hip, Hooray!

_____

is marching toward success in

_____

Signed: _____

Beehive

This cut and paste activity gives the certificate dimension.

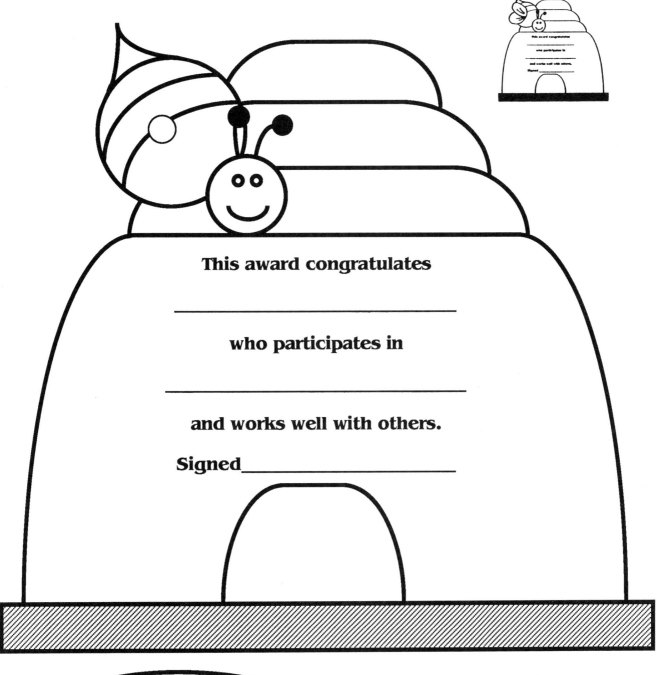

This award congratulates

_____

who participates in

_____

and works well with others.

Signed_____

Bee Wing Pattern

Directions:
- Cut out the hive.
- Trace wing on yellow tissue. Cut out.
- Fold and pinch it on the dotted line.
- Glue the wing to the circle on the large bee.

Bunny

Reproduce on heavy white paper. Color, cut out and fill in the bunny certificate. Ask a child to color, cut and fold the butterfly to paste to the bunny's nose.

Bunny is so pleased that

_____

is _____ in class.

Tickle Bunny's nose with this butterfly.

Signed _____

Snowflake

Make two copies of the pattern for each certificate. Cut out areas with type on one flake. Put it on top of the certificate and attach with a brad in the center. Turn the top snowflake to see the message.

Circus

Reproduce on heavy paper. Fill in the award and punch holes on the small black circles. Tuck a 24" piece of thin yarn or ribbon in with this award for child to sew around the circus wagon.

Ladies and Gentlemen!

_____

has proved that "practice makes perfect" in

_____

and is ready to move on to even
more exciting things in

_____

Signed _____

Rodeo

White the out pony tail to make a boy cowpoke. Reproduce on tan paper and provide coarse string for the cow puncher's rope to glue over the border.

_____

is a Bronco Buster in

_____

Way to go, cowpoke!

Signed: _____

Dinosaurs

You are not "Extinct".
You're "Distinctly" a HUGE success in

_____

Congratulations to

_____

Globe

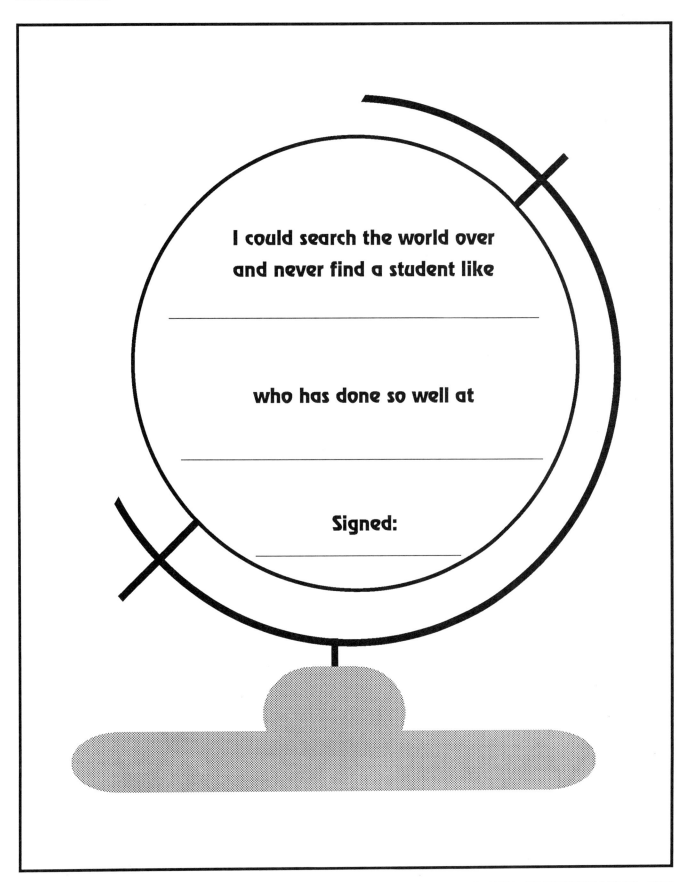

I could search the world over
and never find a student like

_____

who has done so well at

_____

Signed:

_____

Guitar

Reproduce and mount on sturdy paper. Fill in the certificate. Cut out and add yarn or fabric strips for hanging.

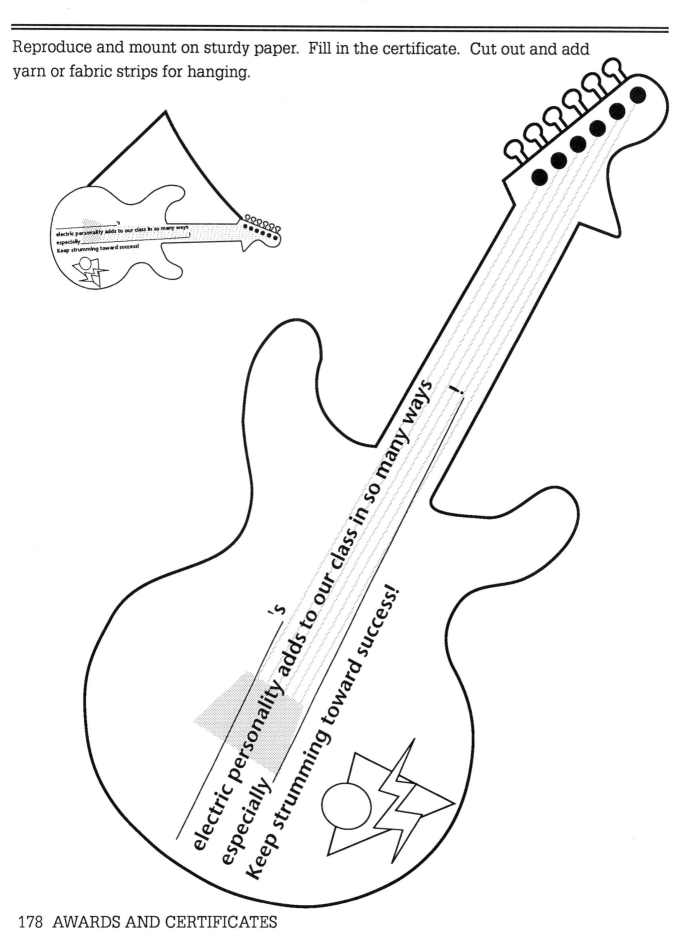

's

electric personality adds to our class in so many ways

especially

Keep strumming toward success!

Star Mobile

Reproduce on sturdy paper and fill in the certificate. Cut along heavy lines. Cut inside star and turn gently to make a dimensional star.

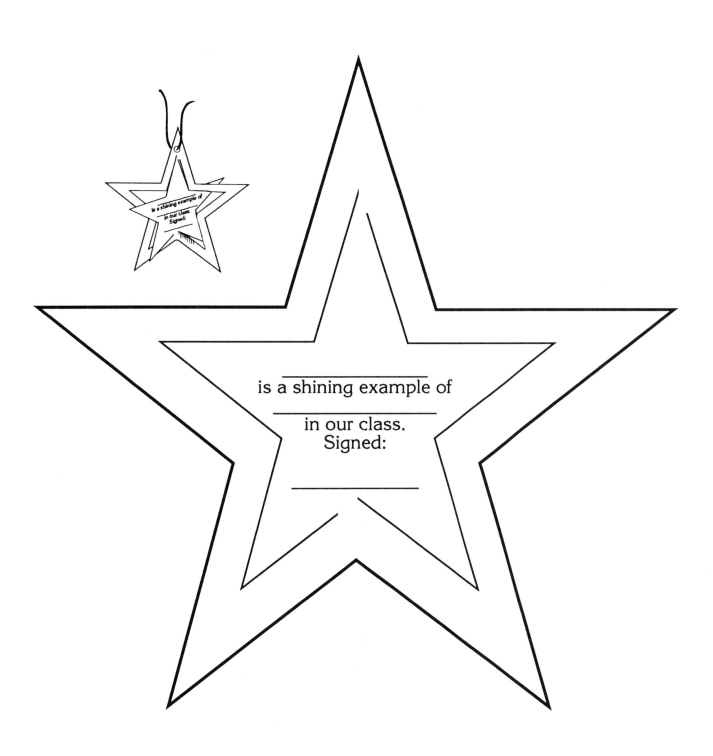

is a shining example of

in our class.
Signed:

Spiral Mobile

Reproduce on pastel colored paper and fill in the certificate. Cut around dotted lines to make a spiral mobile. The child will be able to read the award when the mobile is laid flat and hang it with pride as a reminder of achievement.

is an all around good student in

_____

I'm very pleased with your work. Hang this note in a special place to remind you that I'm happy to have you in my class.

Signed: _____

Mountain Climber

Use string or fine yarn to attach the mountain climber to the mountain. Lace string through the climber as shown. Next put ends of string through holes in the mountain and tape or glue on the back. Move mountain climber up string to reach the top.

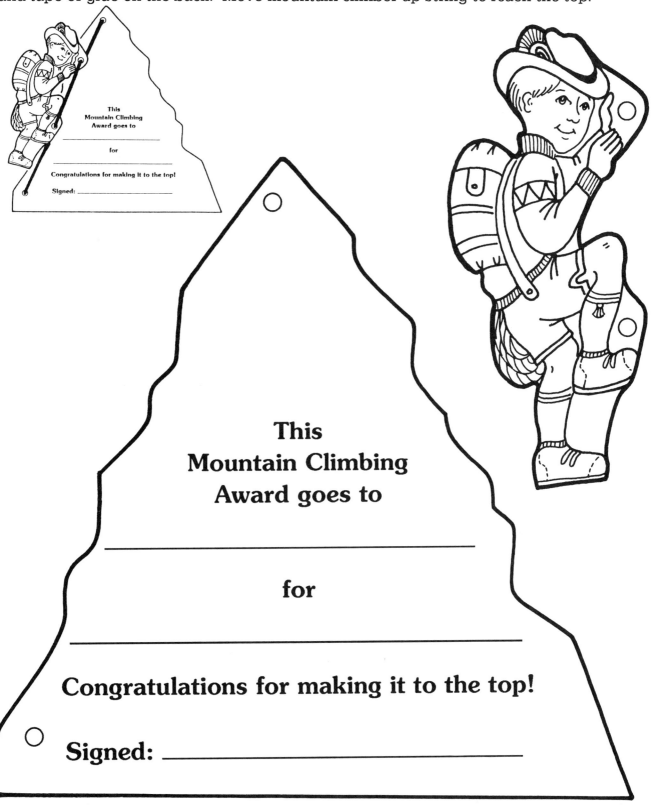

This
Mountain Climbing
Award goes to

_____

for

_____

Congratulations for making it to the top!

○ **Signed:** _____

Peacock

Reproduce certificate on colored paper and fill it in. Give students a dime-sized sequin to glue to the center feather.

should be proud as a peacock because

Santa's Reindeer

Use this certificate to reward any winter holiday project. Reproduce, fill in the blanks and cut out. You may want to glue a red piece of candy on the reindeer's nose.

Ho, ho, ho!
Santa and I know

_____

has been doing a great job at

_____

Signed: _____

Seal of Approval

Reproduce, color and cut out. Glue a round piece of wrapped candy under the ball as a surprise for children receiving this award. Glue both to the tip of the seal's paw.

Seal of Approval
for

_____

who is achieving

_____

in _____

Signed: _____

Ship's Flags

Reproduce on heavy paper. Fill in the certificate. Punch holes in flags and boat. Use a six inch piece of yarn to string flags onto the boat. Tape yarn to the back to secure.

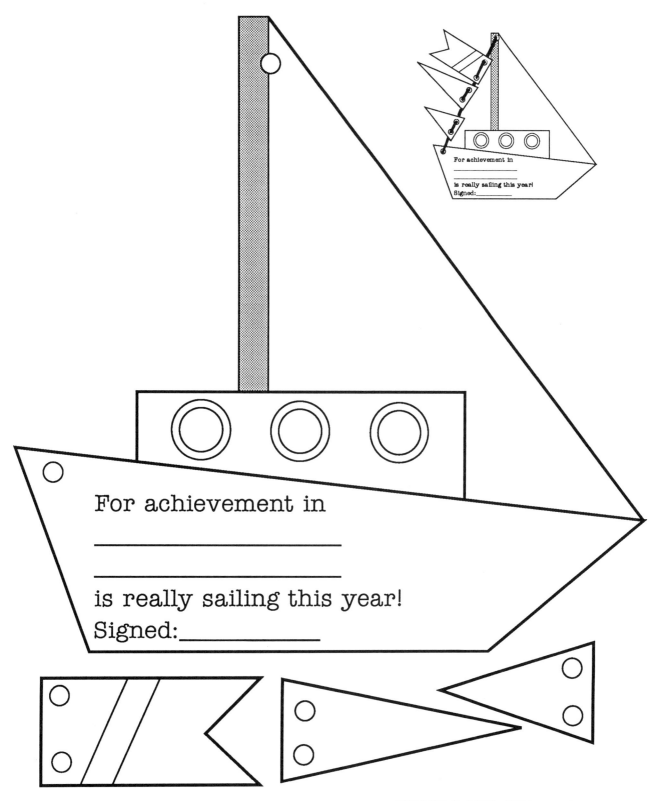

For achievement in

_____

_____

is really sailing this year!
Signed:_____

Space Shuttle

Reproduce the certificate and space shuttle on heavy paper. Use string or fine yarn to attach the space shuttle to the launching tower certificate. Lace string through the shuttle as shown. Next put ends of string through holes in the launching tower and tape or glue on the back. Move shuttle up the string to blast off.

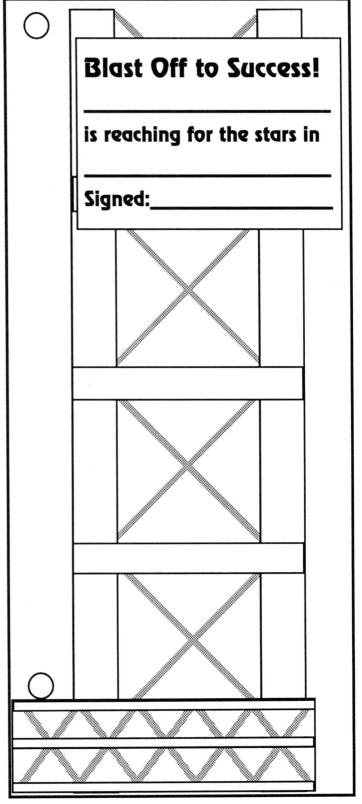

Blast Off to Success!

_____

is reaching for the stars in

_____

Signed:_____

Baseball Bear

Reproduce the bear and cut it out. You may want to tape a piece of gum or wrapped candy on his paw as an extra award.

Baseball Bear and I

are very pleased with

_____'s job on

_____

You deserve a pat on the back

from _____!

Toucan Puzzle

Reproduce, color and cut out the puzzle pieces of the toucan award. Put the pieces into an envelope or clip them together before giving to your achiever to put back together.

Toucan Can and
YOU Can Too!

_____

has shown us how to accomplish goals

with hard work. Great job!

Signed: _____

Whiz Kid Computer

Reproduce the computer terminal on heavy paper and the certificate on plain white paper. Cut the computer screen slits on the heavy lines. Thread the certificate through the slits to read the award message.

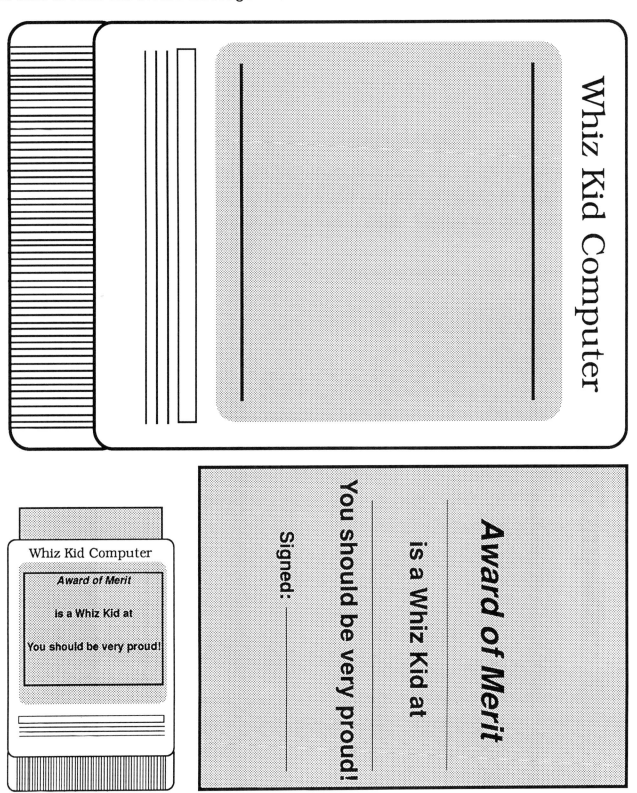

Witch

Reproduce, color and cut out the witch certificate. Tape a candy worm on the witch's hand for a scary treat.

This Bewitching Award

goes to _____

for scaring up a good job in

_____ .

Index

Index